SAUL GOODMAN

MODERN METHOD FOR TYMPANI

by

SAUL GOODMAN

Solo Tympanist, New York Philharmonic Symphony Orchestra,
Instructor of Tympani and Percussion, Juilliard School of Music, New York.

SAUL GOODMAN
1906–1997

Saul Goodman, a native of Brooklyn, New York, began his timpani studies at the age of 14 with Alfred Friese of the New York Philharmonic. In 1926, he was enrolled in a premedical course at New York University when Friese retired due to illness. At the age of 19, Goodman became the orchestra's principal timpanist and served in that position for an unprecedented 46 years, retiring at the end of the 1972 concert season.

Described as a living legend on his instrument, Mr. Goodman has an unparalleled record as a teacher of timpani and percussion. He has students filling posts with most major American orchestras as well as orchestras in Europe and Asia.

Goodman, who also served as the head of the percussion department at the Juilliard School for 41 years, was described as "the Heifetz of the timpani" by *The New York Times* critic Harold Schonberg. He was an accomplished instrument maker and woodworker, building his own drums as well as Leonard Bernstein's batons.

SECTION ONE—Fundamentals

SECTION TWO—Two-Drum Exercises

SECTION THREE—Three- and Four-Drum Exercises

SECTION FOUR—Repertoire for Tympani

Cover Photo by Bert Bial

Thanks to the New York Philharmonic Archives

11424

Arturo Toscanini with Saul Goodman (1936)

Leonard Bernstein with Saul Goodman

Saul Goodman with Igor Stravinsky (1937)

Saul Goodman at Carnegie Hall

ROLAND KOHLOFF

©2000 CHRIS LEE

Roland Kohloff, a native New Yorker, has been principal timpanist of the New York Philharmonic since 1972, the year he succeeded his former teacher, Saul Goodman. Previously, he was the principal timpanist of the San Francisco Symphony and the San Francisco Opera Orchestra, with which he frequently appeared as soloist.

While still a student at the Juilliard School, Mr. Kohloff made his professional debut as a percussion soloist in Stravinsky's *L'Histoire du Soldat* and also appeared with the percussion section of the New York Philharmonic on the famed television program, "Omnibus."

In 1977, Mr. Kohloff gave the New York premiere of Franco Donatoni's Concerto for Strings, Brass and Solo Timpani under the direction of Pierre Boulez and performed with his colleagues in the Philharmonic percussion section in the world premiere of Michael Colgrass's *Déjà vu* for Percussion Quartet and Orchestra, commissioned by the New York Philharmonic. In 1978, he participated in musical history when he played with both the Philharmonic under Zubin Mehta and The Philadelphia Orchestra under Eugene Ormandy the same night. In 1991, he gave the New York premiere of the Timpani Concerto by Siegfried Matthus with the New York Philharmonic. Mr. Kohloff has been a faculty member of the Juilliard School since 1978.

Mr. Kohloff's contributions to the Fundamentals section appear in italics and are based on his study of the material with Saul Goodman.

GARY WERDESHEIM

Gary Werdesheim is Professor of Percussion at the Florida State University School of Music. His training began in San Francisco with Roland Kohloff, followed by three years of repertoire study with Saul Goodman at the Juilliard School in New York City. During those periods he played on many occasions with the San Francisco Symphony, Opera, and Ballet; the New York Philharmonic; and the Metropolitan Opera. For five years he performed at the Aspen Music Festival. He has also taught at the Aspen Music School, the Juilliard School, and Indiana University. Before deciding on a teaching career, he was principal timpanist of the New Jersey Symphony and the Royal Stockholm Philharmonic.

As both player and teacher, Mr. Werdesheim knows the benefits of the proper study and application of the material in this book that has become a bible for so many timpanists and played such an integral part in his own training. From its first printing, however, it contained a disconcerting number of notation and sticking errors, and it has been his long-held desire to do something about it. He was asked to correct the errors, to offer alternatives to some of Mr. Goodman's stickings, and where it seemed helpful, to provide stickings where none were originally indicated.

Mr. Werdesheim believes that stickings, like bowings and fingerings, are a matter of personal preference and are meant to serve one's musical intentions. He encourages students to use his stickings as a guide until they develop an efficient technique and discover their own patterns of technical expression.

Mr. Werdesheim's stickings appear in non-bold italics.

TABLE OF CONTENTS

Introduction 5
The History of Kettledrums 5
Valuation of Notes and Rests 6
Terms, Abbreviations and Signs 8
SECTION ONE – Fundamentals 9
Tuning Designations 9
Foreign Terms 9
Care and Maintenance of the Tympani 10
Type of Tympani Stick to be Used 10
Method of Tucking the Tympani Head 11
Range of the Tympani 12
Tympani Sticks 13
Training the Ear 14
Tuning the Tympani 16
Tuning with the Pedal Tympani 17
Method of Changing the Pitch 18
Arrangement of the Tympani 20
Holding the Sticks 21
Striking the Tympani 22
The Proper Method of Execution 22
Moving From One Drum to Another 24
The Roll 26
The Speed of the Roll 26
Different Types of Rolls 27
The Tied and Separated Roll 28
Muffling the Tympani 31
General Rules to be Followed in Muffling ... 32
The Loud Roll 33
The Forte Piano (fp) Roll 34
Dynamic Control 35
Cross Sticking 36
The Left-Hand Cross 37
The Staccato Stroke 40
The Single, Double and Triple Grace Note .. 42
The Quadruple Grace Note 43
Counting Rests 44
SECTION TWO – Two Drum Exercises 46
SECTION THREE – Three and Four Drums... 61
Three Drum Exercises 62
Four Drum Exercises 67
Technique with the Pedal Tympani 69
Five Drum Study 72
SECTION FOUR – Repertoire for Tympani. 73
Symphony No. 101 (Haydn) 73
Symphony No. 5 (Beethoven) 76
Symphony No. 7 (Beethoven) 80
Symphony No. 9 (Beethoven) 84
Symphony No. 4 (Mendelssohn-Bartholdy).. 90
Symphony No. 1 (Brahms) 93
Symphony No. 4 (Brahms)........................... 98
Symphony No. 4 (Tschaikowsky) 103
Symphony No. 5 (Tschaikowsky) 109
Finlandia (Sibelius) 117
Funeral Music (Wagner) 118
Symphonie Fantastique 119
Till Eulenspiegels (R. Strauss)..................... 120
Schelomo (Bloch)... 123
L'Oiseau de Feu (Strawinsky)....................... 124
Concerto for Violin (Hindemith).................. 126
A Stopwatch and an Ordnance Man (Barber)127
William Billings Overture (W. Schuman)..... 129
American Salute (Gould) 130
Theme and Variations (Goodman)................ 131
Timpiana (Goodman) 132

Introduction

The purpose of this book is to present in a progressive sequence, the materials which are necessary for the training and development of the modern Tympanist.

The book is divided into four sections as follows:

Section 1. The fundamentals of Tympani.
Section 2. Graded exercises for the development of technique on two drums.
Section 3. The technique of three and more drums, and technique with the pedal Tympani.
Section 4. Orchestral studies and solos.

The development of the Tympani has progressed by leaps and bounds during the last twenty years. In addition to the many complex rhythms of modern composers, the tympanist is now confronted with every conceivable type of effect, as a result of the free use of the pedal drums and the demands made on the player by both composer and conductor. It is apparent that the modern tympanist must be a good musician.

The satisfaction of being a proficient Tympanist is without equal, for the Tympanist's position in the orchestra is unique. In fact, he is often called the "Second Conductor," for no other instrument has the range of dynamic power which the proficient Tympanist controls so precisely.

The method of playing no other instrument in the orchestra has caused such controversy as the method of playing the tympani. The methods used in playing it are as many as there are players. Certain similarities do exist, of course, but actually the method used is as individual as the player himself.

Whether or not one agrees with any particular system, the important thing to remember is the results obtained with it. The method used by the author has achieved results of the highest order. In the following pages it will be developed so that the student will have a most complete and orderly conception of the Tympani.

The History Of The Kettle Drums

The first record of the use of the kettledrums goes back to ancient times when it is known that they were used in religious ceremonies by the Hebrews. Whether the kettledrums of this period had any definite pitch is not recorded.

The word tympanum comes from the Greek which means to strike.

In ancient Persia the kettledrums were used to hunt wild birds, the violent striking of the drums causing the birds to fly about enabling the huntsmen to shoot them down.

The glamorous period of kettledruming existed during the middle ages when kettledrummers formed themselves into a guild, the entry into which called for a long period of apprenticeship. At this time the most honorable privilege of the kettledrummer was to participate at the tournaments of the knights and nobles.

During the seventeenth century kettledrums received their first musical distinction by being used with the trumpets to punctuate the tonic and dominant of the key and to give rythmical support to the music.

Beethoven was the first composer to radically change the tuning of the drums by startling the musical world with the tuning of the drums in octaves in the eighth and ninth symphonies.

Hector Berlioz realized the further possibilities of the instruments by tuning them in thirds and fifths thus creating an entire chord with the drums. In the Symphony Fantastique, four kettledrums differently tuned are used to create the effect of distant thunder.

Most composers of this period realized the harmonic value of the drums but due to the mechanical limitations of the instruments then in use, often neglected to indicate changes of intonation and as a result the Tympani were used often as a percussive effect without any harmonic value whatsoever.

Richard Wagner saw the tremendous dramatic effects obtainable with the kettledrums. In several of the Ring operas two players are used with many important parts assigned to them.

With the advent of the pedal Tympani composers have run rampant with the drums and today the drums not only have rhythmical and harmonic value, but are often called upon to play actual melodies with the most startling effects thus obtained.

Valuation Of Notes And Rests

Here is given a diagram showing the proper way of dividing a whole note.

The whole note or 4 quarters

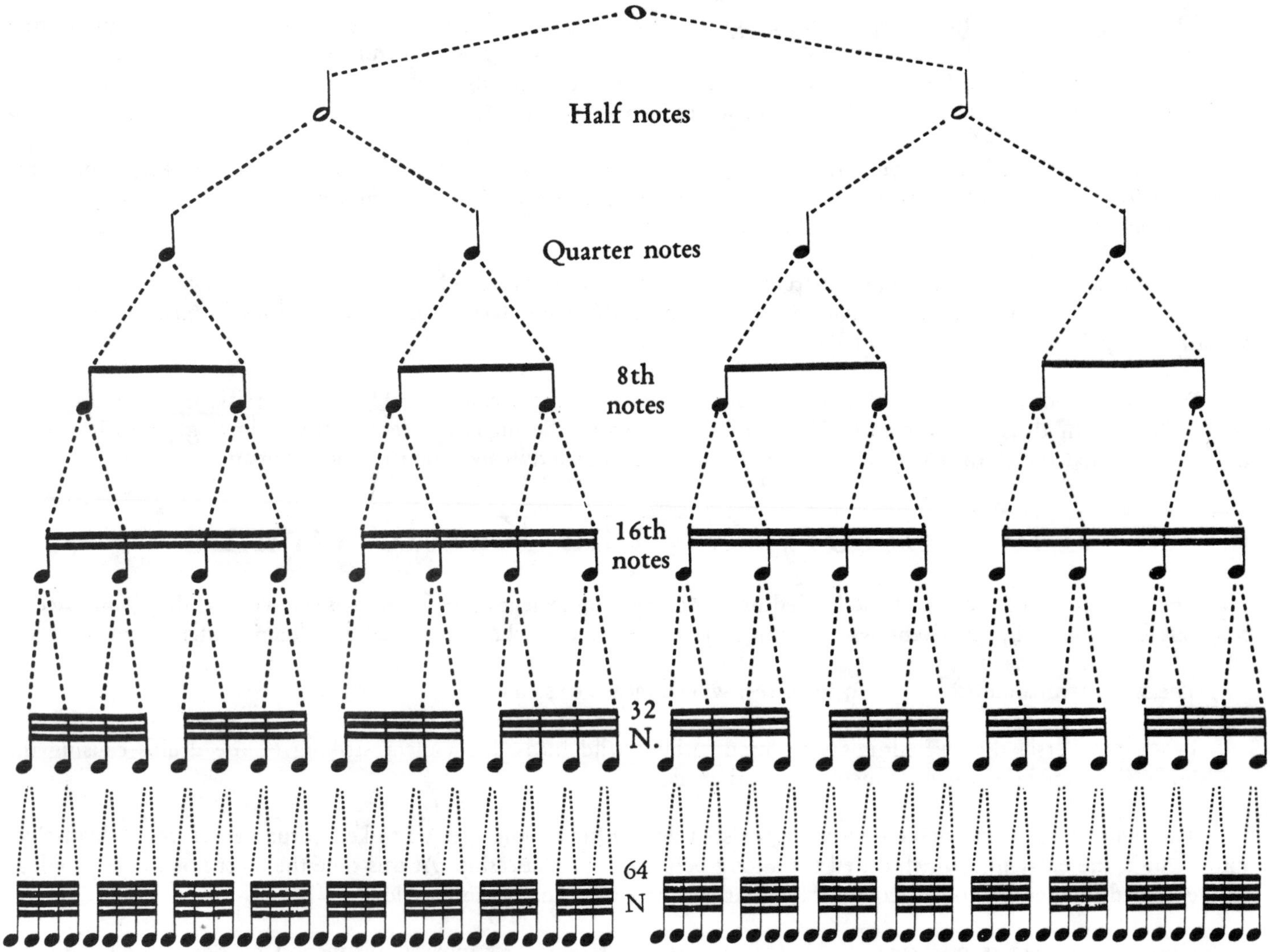

Half notes

Quarter notes

8th notes

16th notes

32 N.

64 N

This is how 8th, 16th, 32nd and 64th notes appear when written separately (not in group form.)

RESTS

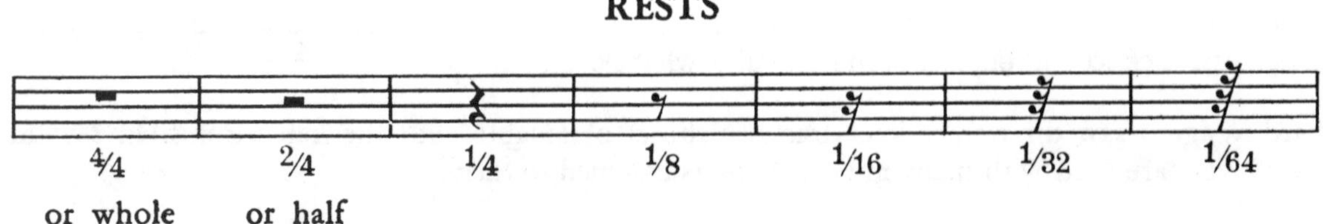

A dot placed after a note or rest increases its value by one-half

Two dots after a note or rest increases its value by three-fourths

Artificial groups of notes which are played in other than their original form

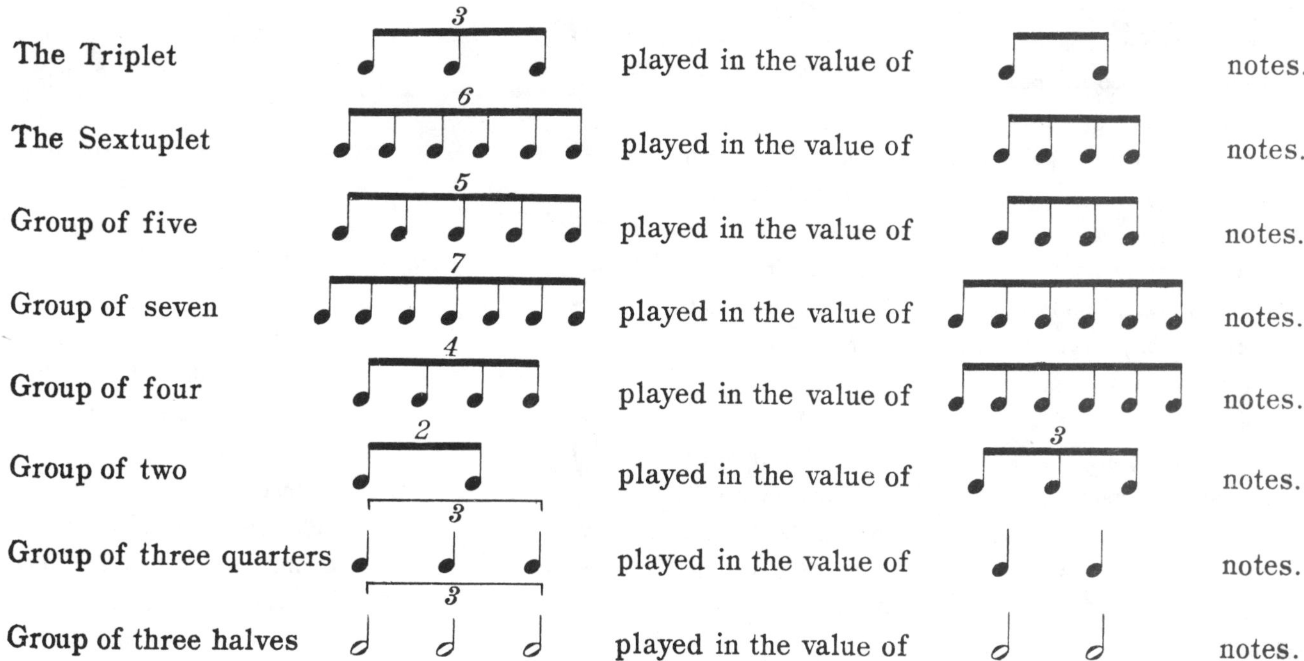

Terms, Abbreviations And Signs

TERMS

Accelerando (ät-cha-le-*rän*-do)	Gradually faster
Adagio (a-*dä*-jó)	Very slowly
Ad libitum (äd-*lib*-i-tum)	At liberty
Allargando (al-lär-*gän*-do)	Broadening out
Allegretto (al-le-*gret*-to)	Moderately fast
Allegro (ä-*la*-gro)	Quick, lively
Andante (an-*dän*-ta)	Moderately slow
Andantino (än-dän-*te*-no)	A little faster than andante
Animato (än-e-*mä*-to)	With animation
A tempo (ä *tem*-po)	At the original rate of speed
Bis (bis)	Repeat measure
Chromatic (kro-*mat*-ik)	Proceeding by half tones
Coda (*ko*-dä)	A number of measures used to close a composition
Con brio (kon *bré*-o)	With life and fire
Con moto (kon-*mo*-to)	With motion; not dragging
Con spirito (kon *spe*-re-to)	With spirit
Crescendo (kre-*shen*-do)	Gradually louder
Da Capo (dä *kä*-po)	Return to the beginning
Dal segno (däl *sa*-yno)	From the sign
Decrescendo (da-kre-*shen*-do)	Gradually softer
Diminuendo (de-me-*nwen*-do)	Gradually softer
Fine (*fe*-na)	The end
Forte (*fôr*-ta)	Loud
Fortissimo (fôr-*tis*-i-mo)	Very loud
Forzando (fôr-*tsän*-do)	Accented; with sudden emphasis
Giocoso (je-o-*ko*-zo)	Playfully
Largo (*lär*-go)	Slowly
Legato (le-*gä*-to)	In a smooth, sustained manner
Leggeramente (led-jehr-ä-*men*-ta)	Easily, lightly
Leggero (led-*jer*-o)	Easily, lightly
Leggiere (led-*je*-a-re)	Easily, lightly
Lento (*len*-to)	Slowly
L'istesso tempo (lis-*tes*-so *tem*-po)	In the same time
Maestoso (mä-es-*to*-so)	Majestic, with dignity
Ma non troppo (mä non *tro*-po)	But not too much
Marcato (mar-*kä*-to)	Marked, accented
Marcia (*mar*-che-ä)	In march tempo and style
Meno mosso (ma-no *mos*-so)	Less movement, slower
Mezzo piano (med-zo pi-*a*-no)	Moderately soft
Mezzo forte (med-zo *fôr*-ta)	Moderately loud
Moderato (mod-e-*rä*-to)	Moderately
Molto (*mol*-to)	Very, much
Morendo (mo-*ren*-do)	Dying away
Pianissimo (pe-ä-*nis*-i-mo)	Extremely soft
Piano (pi-*ä*-no)	Smooth, even, soft
Poco a poco (*po*-ko ä *po*-ko)	Little by little
Presto (*pres*-to)	Rapidly, very quick
Prestissimo (*Press*-tiss-i-mo)	Rapidly as possible
Rallentando (räl-en-*tän*-do)	Gradually slower
Ritardando (re-tär-*dän*-do)	Retarding, holding back
Ritenuto (re-te-*noo*-to)	Retarding, holding back
Simile (*sim*-i-le)	Continue in the same way
Sostenuto (Sus-ten-*oo*-to)	Sustained
Staccato (stä-*kä*-to)	Very short
Tempo (*tem*-po)	Time; rate of movement
Tenuto (ta-*noo*-to)	Hold full value or a little over
Tutti (*too*-tê)	All, together
Valse (vals)	A waltz
Vivace (ve-*vä*-cha)	Lively, rapid

ABBREVIATIONS

Abbreviation	Meaning
f	forte, loud
ff	fortissimo, Very loud
fff	fortefortissimo, Extremely loud
fp	forte-piano, Strongly attacked and immediately soft.
mf	mezzo forte, The medium between soft and loud
p	piano, Soft
pp	pianissimo, Very soft
ppp	pianopianissimo, Extremely soft
mp	mezzo piano, Medium between soft and very soft
sfz	sforzando, Very strongly accented
Dim	diminuendo
Rit	ritenuto
Rall	rallentando
M.M. ♩ = 96	An indication of the number of beats per minute
Tr	trill
D. S.	Dal segno
D. C.	Da capo

SIGNS

:‖	Repeat sign; return to this sign ‖: or in its absence to the beginning
‖:	Beginning of a repeated section
𝄐	Fermata, pause, hold; sustain tone beyond its value. Watch the director
<	Crescendo; gradually increase the volume
>	Decrescendo; gradually decrease the volume
>	Accent or stress the tone
𝄌	Coda sign; go directly from this sign to the section marked Coda.
𝄋	Segno; repeat from this sign
♩̣ ♩̣ ♩̣	Staccato; play tones in a disconnected manner and generally one-half of their full value.
8va	Play one octave higher than written
,	Coma, stop slightly before proceeding
♩̱	Sustain the tone to its full value
𝄎	Repeat the preceding measure
𝄏	Repeat the preceding two measures

SECTION ONE

Tuning Designations

The notes to which the tympani are to be tuned are designated in several ways:

At the beginning of the piece to be played may be found the heading TYMPANI in C & F, A & D, etc.

or

a small staff placed at the beginning

or

the key signature placed on the staff

Note: With some modern composers no tuning designation is given, but the notes and their accidentals are indicated as they occur.

Foreign Terms Used To Indicate Notes To Which The Tympani Are To Be Tuned

Naturals	*Italian*	*French*	*German*
F	Fa	Fa	F
G	Sol	Sol	G
A	La	La	A
B	Si	Si	H (Ha)
C	Do	Ut	C
D	Re	Re	D
E	Mi	Mi	E

Accidentals

In Italian or French the word *Bemolle* or *Bemol* means flat and the word *Diesis* or *Diese* means sharp. In German *Fis* means F#, *Ges* means G*b*, *As* means A*b*, *Ha* means B natural, *B* means B*b*, *Cis* means C#, *Des* means D*b* and *Es* means E*b*. Note: With some of the seventeenth century composers, all tympani parts were written in C and G and their tuning designation given at the beginning of the part to be played:

Example

Tympani in D & A

etc.

When these parts are encountered the player should be careful to note the correct tuning of the drums given at the beginning of the part.

Care And Maintenance Of The Tympani

When Tympani are not in use, they should be placed away from heat of any kind. Care should be taken not to relax the tension on the heads entirely or allow too much tension on the head.

If the drums are to be used under extremely damp conditions the heads should be left with a very small amount of tension when not in use.

If the drums are to be used under extremely warm and dry conditions they are best left in the following condition when not in use:

The large drum tuned to B♮. 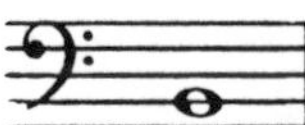 The small drum tuned to E♮. 

This will help in maintaining the "Collar" which is important in order to obtain the lower notes.

When Tympani are not in use the heads should be tuned carefully. This will help to insure clear even intonation when they are to be played on again.

If as a result of extremely dry conditions the Tympani head should have lost it's "collar," the head should be removed from the drum and moistened on both sides, care being taken that the old crease in the head is well softened before the head is replaced on the kettle. Wetting of the head on one side only should be avoided although this may be done with the head on the kettle when sufficient time does not allow wetting both sides.

It should be noted that too much wetting of the head kills the life in the head and often results in making it false and toneless. Proper tucking of the head will greatly assist in stabilizing it and the elimination of unnecessary moistening.

All moving parts should be kept free and screws well oiled.

Type Of Tympani Stick To Be Used

The handles of Tympani sticks are best made from straight grained hickory or rock maple. An elastic type handle is not recommended. A rigid handle helps produce the best tone and a clear concise beat.

The handle itself may be from thirteen to fifteen inches long, depending on the preference of the player.

The recommended type of balls for the stick are the "Cart Wheel" and the "Ball" types.

The Cart Wheel type is constructed as follows:

The hard inner core should be of hard felt about one and one quarter inches in diameter and one inch in thickness. Around this inner core is sewn a thin layer of medium felt the same width as the core. Around this layer is sewn a layer of soft damper felt. This should produce a ball approximately two inches in diameter.

Construction of the "Ball" type stick is as follows:

The inner core should be of wood or hard felt about one inch in diameter and about three quarters of an inch in thickness. Over this core is placed a piece of medium hard felt sewn in the form of a bag and pulled tightly over the core. On top of this is placed the soft damper felt sewn in the form of a bag and pulled tightly over the resulting core. This ball when finished should be about two inches in diameter and one and three quarters to two inches in length.

It should be noted that the larger the ball the greater amount of tone will be produced. However, balls that are too large will produce a stifled sound on the Tympani. A head under extreme dry conditions will need a stick with a large ball to produce the proper amount of resonance. Conversely under damp conditions a smaller ball is recommended because this condition tends to make the head vibrate more freely.

A hard stick should not be used when there is not much vibration in the head. The best type of stick to use for general work is one that will give both tone and clearness.

Sticks For Specialized Use

Wood Sticks (Holz Schlegel, Baguette en Bois) are used to produce piercing and sharp rhythmical effects. This type of stick should be used with the utmost discretion and only where indicated by the composer. A small wooden ball one inch in diameter and one inch in thickness mounted on a regular Tympani stick handle is sufficient.

For very fast passages that are to be played very softly, a stick with a very small ball is recommended. To further prevent the vibrations of the head from interfering with the clarity of the beat, placing a small piece of soft felt or a handkerchief on the head where it adjoins the rim, will help in making the beats clearer.

Method Of Tucking The Tympani Head

Before tucking the Tympani head it should be determined beforehand whenever possible under what conditions (dampness, dryness, heat, etc.) the head will be subjected to, when in use. For example, if the head is to be used under extreme dry conditions it should be tucked with a large amount of slack. If on the other hand the head is to be used under extreme damp conditions it is recommended to tuck the head flush eliminating all the slack.

Under moderate conditions it is best at all times to allow a small amount of slack in order to compensate for slight changes of conditions in either direction.

1. Soak the head in cool water (about 65 degrees F.) for about thirty minutes until it is soft and pliable. A heavier head will require a little longer soaking than a thinner one. Care should be taken not to soak the head in water that is too cold or too warm. Over soaking the head will cause it to lose its finish and bring on the appearance of white spots (in a transparent head).

2. After the head has been soaked for the proper amount of time spread it out on a large table which has been covered with paper. With a soft cloth remove all surplus water, first on one side, then on the other.

3. Determine the beating side of the head by the one having the smoothest texture. Most American made heads have the manufacturers stamp on the beating side.

4. Place the head on the table with the beating side facing the table. (If the head is to be put on reversed, the beating side should be placed face upward)

5. Regulate the amount of slack in the head by placing a wooden bowl (or a ball made from paper) under the exact center. Make sure that the backbone of the head is in the exact center.

6. Place the flesh hoop on the top of the head so that at least two inches of the head project beyond this hoop, Slightly more than this amount may be needed depending on the thickness of the flesh hoop used.

7. Use a standard tucking tool or the back end of a rounded spoon handle. Fold over a small portion of the head over the flesh hoop and with the tucking tool force it under the flesh hoop. It is best to tuck opposite sides by first dividing the hoop into four equal parts and then continue with opposite sides until the entire head has been tucked under the hoop.

8. Allow the head to dry in a dry cool place entirely free of heat for about one hour. Before placing the head on the kettle rub the rim of the kettle with a piece of paraffin or wax.

9. Place the head on the kettle and attach counter hoop and screws. Pull the head down with the screws so that about one quarter to one half inch of collar is obtained.

10. Allow to dry in a cool place away from heat for about thirty six hours. More or less time may be required depending on drying conditions.

Note: The head may also be allowed to dry completely on the flesh hoop before being placed on the kettle. If this method is used the head should be moistened on both sides before being placed on the kettle.

Range Of The Tympani

The tympani sound as written. They are non-transposing instruments.

The complete range of the modern tympani is from low C to high C.

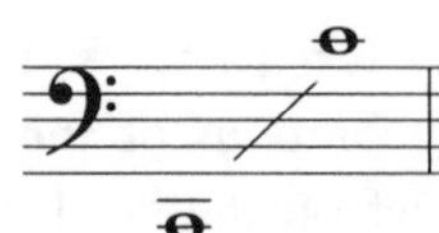

The correct size drum should be used whenever possible in order to get a good quality sound for each note. The most popular size drums are the 28" and the 25".

The large 28" drum has a range from low F to C.

The smaller 25" drum has a range from B♭ to F.

It is possible, and sometimes practical, to go above or below the given range for these drums. These notes are not recommended for the given sizes and should only be used when necessary.

The large drum (28") can produce the low E and high D.

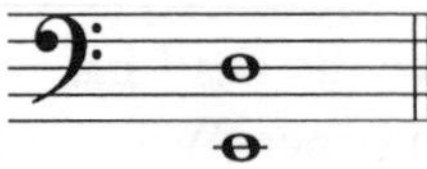

The small drum (25") can produce the low A♭ and the high G.

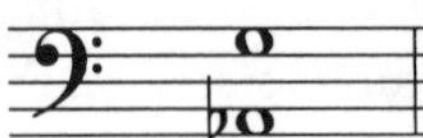

The 30" or 32" drum will give good quality from low C to A.
The low C will need a drum of 32" or larger to obtain a high quality sound.

The 23" drum will give good quality from high D to A.

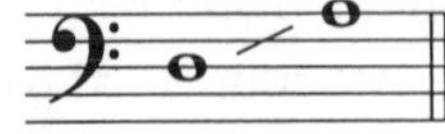

The piccolo drum of 22" or smaller, will give a good quality from the high F to the C above.

Several of the modern composers have used the extreme ranges of the tympani very effectively. Janacěk used the high B♭, and Stravinsky used the high B♮. The celebrated conductor, Stokowski, in his orchestral transcriptions of Bach, used the low C.

Tympani Sticks

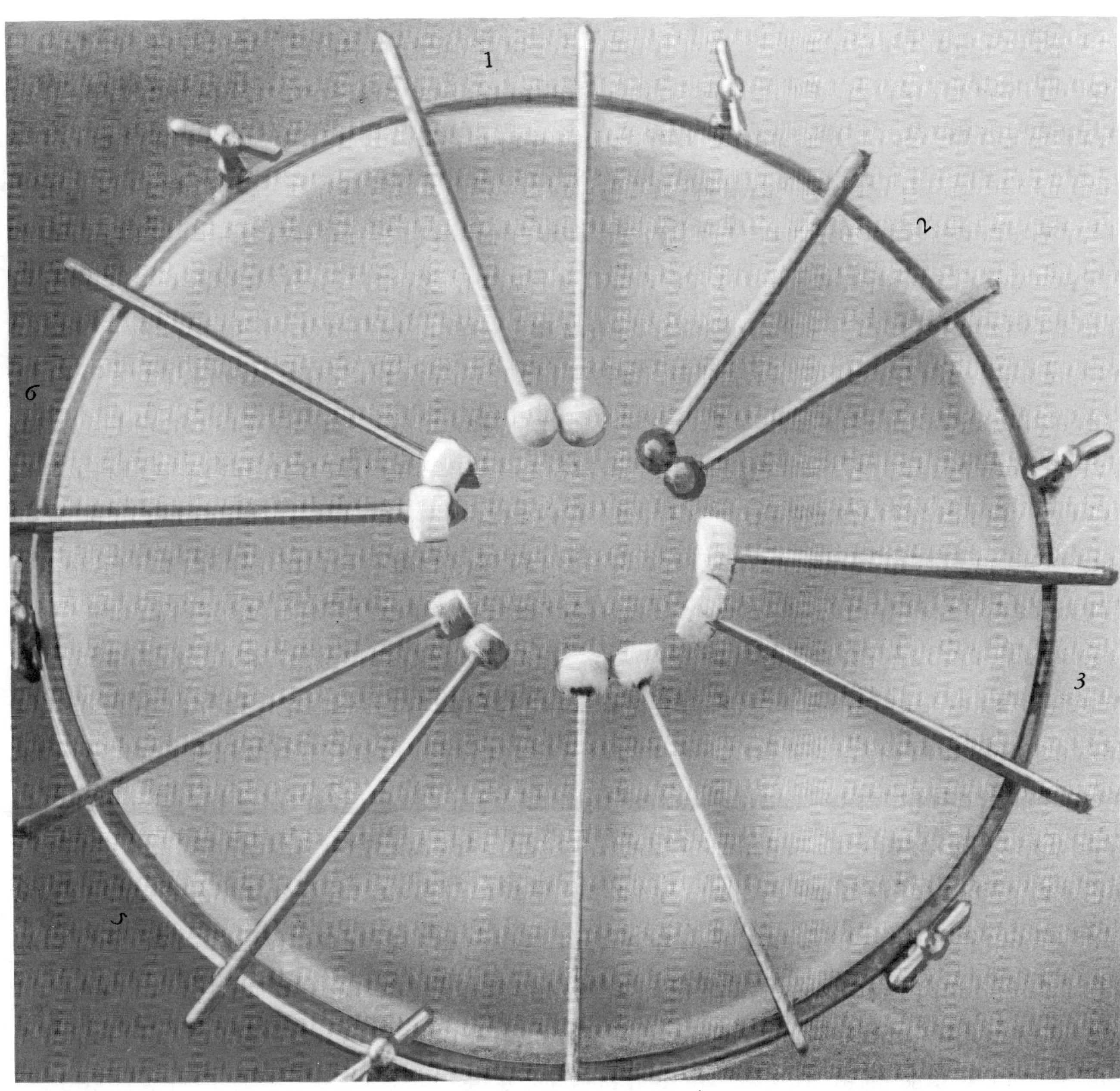

NO.	NAME OF STICK	RECOMMENDED USE
1.	Small Headed Sticks	Staccato and precise rhythmical effects.
2.	Wooden Sticks	Specialized rhythmical effects as indicated by the composer.
3.	Cartwheel Type Sticks	General use and tone.
4.	Light Small Headed Sticks	Soft Staccato work.
5.	Flannel Headed Sticks	Extremely soft staccato work.
6.	Ball Type Stick	All around general use.

Training The Ear In Preparation For Tuning The Tympani

The actual process of training the ear for tuning the Tympani depends largely on the musical background of the student. For those students who already play some musical instrument, it will be relatively simple to learn the necessary fundamentals of tuning. For those students whose musical background is limited the following method will serve to develop the ear.

The main basis of tuning the Tympani is a thorough knowledge of intervals. The following are the more important intervals with their number of steps and half steps which determines the interval.

The minor second	=	1 half step
The major second	=	1 full step
The minor third	=	1½ steps
The major third	=	2 steps
The perfect fourth	=	2½ steps
The augmented fourth or diminished fifth	=	3 steps
The perfect fifth	=	3½ steps
The minor sixth	=	4 steps
The major sixth	=	4½ steps
The minor seventh or dim. seventh	=	5 steps
The major seventh	=	5½ steps
The octave	=	6 steps

These intervals will serve as the most practical in tuning the Tympani.

It will be most helpful for the student if he will secure for himself an A-440 tuning fork or pitch pipe and sound this note to himself at odd moments. It is surprising how quickly this note can be sung from memory. The acquiring of this asset will be most helpful in tuning the Tympani.

TABLE I

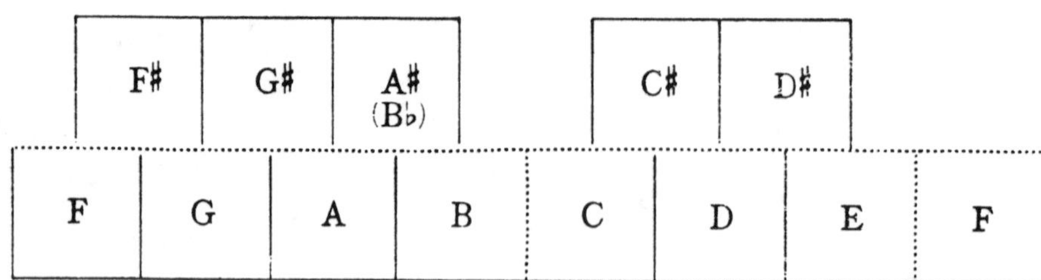

In table I it will be noted that there are solid lines and dotted lines. When the solid line is crossed in going from one tone to another let us call it a full step or whole tone. When the dotted line is crossed in going from one tone to another let us call it a half step or half tone.

Thus in going from A to B we cross one solid line. In doing this we have progressed one step or one full tone above A. Looking at our formula we find that one full step equals a major second. Therefore the interval between A and B is a major second.

If we go from A to A# (Sharp) we only progress one half step above A. Looking at the formula we find that one half step equals a minor Second, since we cross one dotted line.

By using this method the student who is not familiar with intervals can tell at a glance, by using table I and the formula, the actual name of the interval before determining its sound.

Having determined the interval by name we can now proceed to determine it's actual sound.

The use of some musical instrument (preferably a Piano) is recommended in hearing the actual sound of the interval.

Take the minor second for example. From our formula we know that the minor second is one half step above or below a given note.

Thus looking at table I if we cross over from A to A# we cross the dotted line or progress one half step. Go to the Piano, Orchestra bells, Xylophone (or even a well tuned pitch pipe can be used) and get the sound of this combination. Sing it to yourself aloud and then try to fix the interval firmly in your mind. Now try other combinations of minor seconds using table I to locate them.

Try doing the same thing using the formula for the major second. Proceed then to the minor third and then locate all the intervals given in the table of formulae. Get the sound of these intervals firmly fixed in your ear.

Do not try to learn too many intervals at one time. It is best to set a schedule for yourself of one or two intervals at a time and learn them thoroughly.

In singing the intervals to yourself it will be found helpful to use the syllable Ba. This forces the mouth open and produces a more accurate pitch.

Since the ear is a very sensitive organ it is better to practice this type of ear training no longer than an hour at a time. When the ear becomes tired it is inaccurate in pitch. This is something that the student should avoid, since it is essential in tuning the drums to work for accuracy.

The student should get used to seeing the intervals and hearing them in the Bass clef since this is the clef that is used for the Tympani.

The following are the intervals as they look and sound:

It will be noted that the intervals given are those which actually exist and are possible within the range of the Tympani. The student should be able to recognize these intervals in all other clefs and positions where they might occur. After mastering these fundamental intervals it should be relatively simple to locate any interval no matter where it might occur.

It cannot be too strongly emphasized to learn these intervals most thoroughly. This knowledge will become the main basis for tuning the Tympani.

Tuning The Tympani

The most frequent intervals that occur in tuning the Tympani are the perfect fourth and the perfect fifth. The student should make a special point of recognizing these intervals.

If you have learned your intervals well the actual tuning of the drums should not be too difficult.

It is best to learn to tune the drums with the sticks in one hand as shown in the photo below.

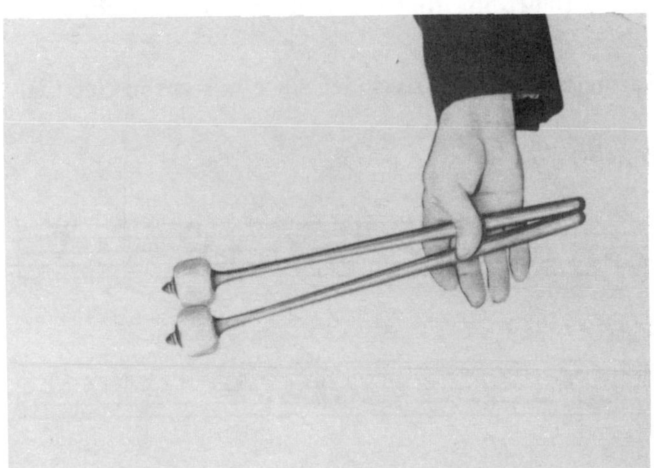

At this time do not attempt to tune the drums by flipping with the finger. This method is unsatisfactory for the student since when striking the drum with the stick after tuning with the finger the same pitch is not produced.

If the hand Tympani are used, learn to turn the screws in pairs using the two screws nearest you, then the center pair and finally the farthest pair.

Before you are ready to tune, first sing the note you desire to yourself. Tap the drum and decide for yourself whether the drum is too high or too low. After you have made your decision, proceed to make the necessary adjustment either tightening or loosening the screws, whichever you have found necessary. After this adjustment is made sing the note desired to yourself once again and compare it to the pitch of the drum. By repeating this process you will get the note desired. Do not attempt to sing at the same time that you are testing the drum to ascertain it's pitch. SING THE NOTE TO YOURSELF FIRST, AND THEN TAP THE DRUM AND CONCENTRATE ON THE PITCH OBTAINED.

In tuning a given interval, first obtain one note and then sing the interval desired from the note thus obtained. Do not try to tune the notes desired by conceiving of them individually. Remember that what you are primarily interested in is to obtain THE INTERVAL RELATIONSHIP BETWEEN THE TWO TONES. For example if it is desired to tune the Tympani in A and D,

Tune the A or D first, whichever you choose, and then sing a fourth above or below whichever note you have obtained first. If one of the notes is tuned accurately and then the interval sung correctly, the tuning of the desired interval should be correct.

Tuning With The Pedal Tympani

Tuning with the pedal type tympani makes for greater accuracy because it creates an immediate equal tension on the head. The possibilities of rapid tuning are almost limitless with the pedal tympani.

Although the pedal drum is the ideal instrument to use, nevertheless a real understanding of the characteristics of the head are best acquired by a thorough knowledge of the hand tympani.

Practically all pedal tympani operate on the same principle. By pushing the pedal forward or (downward), the tone is raised. By releasing the pedal, the tone is lowered.

On American made instruments, all the fine adjustments are made with the six or eight hand screws. With modern pedal tympani, the fine adjustments are made with a master screw or handle that adjusts the tension with one operation.

Before beginning to tune the pedal tympani, make sure the lowest tones are as follows:

On the large drum (28"), the tone should be low F.
The top range of this drum should be at least the C above.

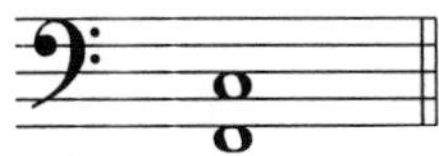

On the small drum (25"), the lowest tone should be the low B♭.
The top note will then be the high F above.

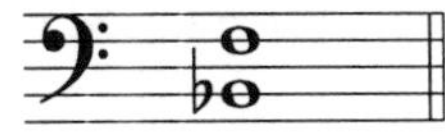

When the range on the drums have been set, use the following method for tuning the pedal tympani:

1. A beginner may wish to start by using a pitch pipe to hear the note. However, eventually the student should advance to using a tuning fork to find the desired note.

2. Sing the desired pitch.

3. Singing is fine, if accurate. If the student cannot sing on pitch, I recommend tuning by listening.

4. Release the pedal, strike the drum lightly with the stick and immediately slide up to the note by pushing the pedal forward. If the first attempt has not been successful, repeat the operation.

5. Check the pitch by using a piano, marimba or vibraphone, if possible.

In tuning, it is always best to go below the note desired and tune up to it. This will eliminate any tendency of the head to stick and will produce more accurate intonation.

Method Of Changing The Pitch Of The Drums From Intervals Already Established

Method of Changing the pitch of the drums from intervals already established.

For example:

If the drums are already tuned in A and D

and it is desired to tune them to F# and C#:

Referring to table 1 it is noted that the jump downward from A to F# is one and one half steps. This equals a minor third as given in the formula. We therefore sing down a minor third. In doing this the F# is obtained. Now going from F# to C# we count three and a half steps. This we know from the formula is a perfect fifth. By singing up a perfect fifth from F# we thus obtain C#. The drums are now tuned in F# and C#.

The same result may be obtained by singing up a major third above A. This will produce the C#, and by singing down a fifth from the C#, the F# is obtained.

It is also possible to sing down a minor second from D to C#, and then a fifth down to F#. Any of these methods is correct, depending on the preference of the student as to which one he would like to use.

The same method can be used in going from F# and C#

To B and E.

From F# to B is two and one half steps or a perfect fourth. By singing up a fourth from F# the B is obtained. E is two and one half steps above B, therefore a fourth above. In this manner the interval B and E are obtained.

By using this method the task of the student in moving from one set of intervals to another is simplified.

Method Of Changing The Pitch Of The Drums From The Fixed Note A

It has already been recommended that the student memorize the note A. When this note has been firmly established in the mind, any interval or combination of intervals may be obtained from it.

For example; If it is desired to tune the Tympani in C and F,

sing the note A.

From A to C is one and one half steps or a minor third.

By singing a minor third above A, the note C is obtained. The F above C is two and one half steps or a perfect fourth. Therefore, we arrive at the interval C and F.

Similarly, if it is desired to tune C# and G#, C# is a major third above A. Having obtained the C#, sing down a fourth to arrive at G#.

Practice tuning the following intervals by the method below:

1. *Tune 1st measure.*
2. *Check the pitches for accuracy and adjust if necessary.*
3. *Proceed to the next measure and repeat the procedure.*

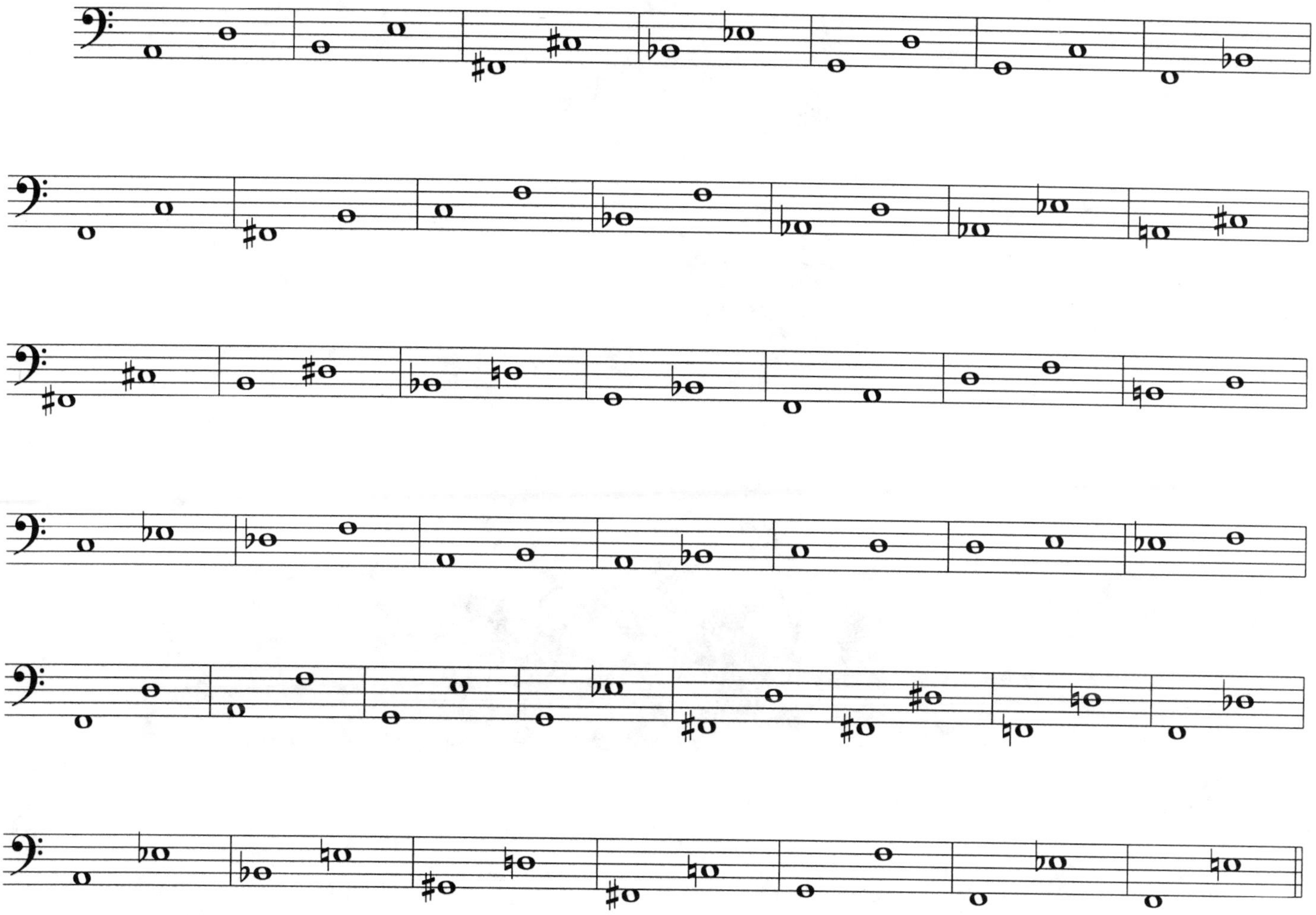

Try playing the above exercise as written below:

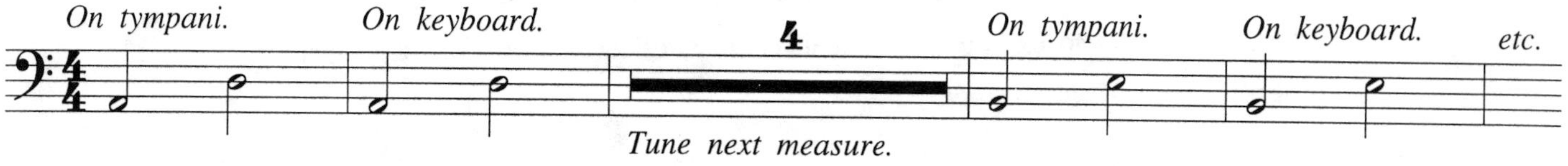

On tympani. *On keyboard.* 4 *On tympani.* *On keyboard.* *etc.*

Tune next measure.

Arrangement Of The Tympani

The Tympani should be placed so that the small drum is on the right and the large drum on the left. The drums should be horizontal not tilted.

1. The drums should be about eight inches below the players waist.

2. The player should be in a standing position so that the mid line of the body coincides with the spot where one drum adjoins the other.

3. The feet should be not too far apart or too close together. The feet should be as in a normal standing position. The player should have the feeling of complete freedom of motion.

4. The movement from one drum to another is from the waist.

NOTE

Although it is possible to play the tympani in a sitting position, playing the instrument in this manner does not make for freedom of motion which is most important for proper execution. The player should, at all times, avoid a sitting position. It should be noted, however, that in playing the Pedal Tympani, it is essential, in order to execute the difficult changes of intonation, for the player to rest his body against a stool.

Holding The Sticks

Before beginning the preliminary exercises, it is absolutely essential that the student understand and master the correct method of holding the sticks. Only then will he/she be able to go on and master the principles of setting the hands in motion to execute the fundamental single stroke.

The author's entire technique is based upon this method of holding the sticks. The student must, therefore, make every effort to acquire, as soon as possible, the habit of holding the tympani sticks in this way.

First, study all the photos in this section carefully; then try it by holding the sticks. Getting the position correct from the very start will save a lot of trouble later.

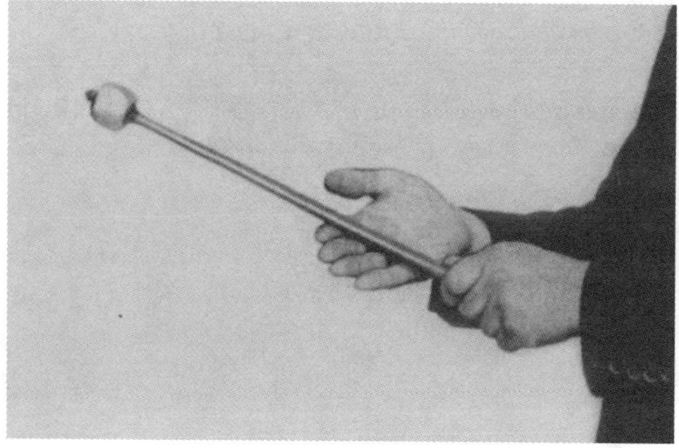

Right hand palm up, fingers extended.
Stick laid across the first joint of the index finger, about 3 inches from the end of the stick.

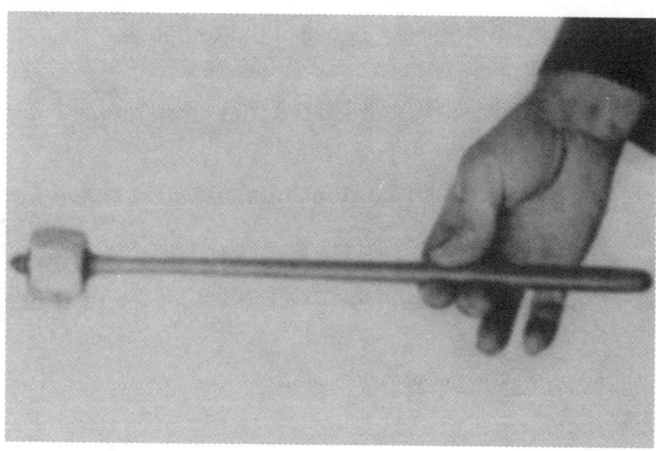

Place the thumb on the stick and in line with the stick.

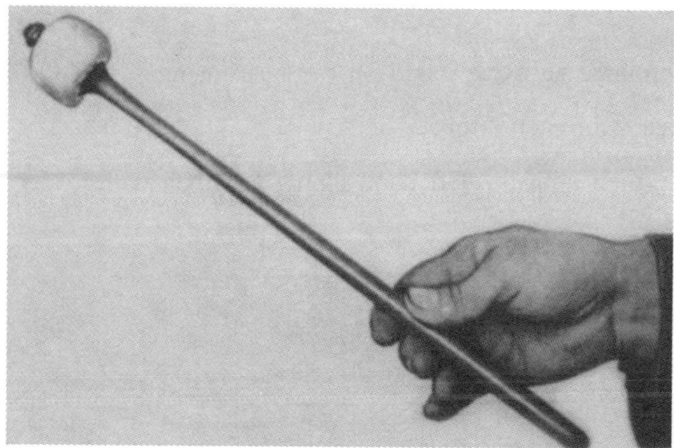

Curl the 2nd and 3rd fingers underneath the stick gently. The 4th or little finger should not come into contact with the stick at all.

Turn the hand over so the thumb is resting on the side of the stick. Rest the stick on the drum head, 3 to 4 inches from the rim.

Do the same with the left hand. Make certain that every detail is correct.

When both sticks are held in this fashion, the general position of the body is as in the photo. Notice how the elbows project slightly from the sides of the body and how the sticks form a "V" open at the end.

The beating spot—the place where the head is struck—should be 3 to 4 inches from the rim of the drum.

Striking The Tympani

It is important to remember that the tympani should be struck in the same area of the head each time. If this is not done, a variety of uneven sounds are produced.

The motion used in striking the tympani is that of wrist and fingers. No arm or elbow motion is used at this time. In order to understand this properly, do the following:

1. Rest the stick on the drum head, 3 to 4 inches from the rim.

2. Grip the stick firmly between the thumb and first finger. *Curl the second and third fingers around the stick.*

3. With the wrist only, raise the stick upwards *and strike the drum in a downward motion.*

4. When the stick strikes the drum, *the hand catches it as it rebounds.*

This procedure should be practiced with alternate hands: right, left, right, left.

The Proper Method Of Execution

It is essential that the player equalize the strokes in order to produce an even sound on the instrument.

Make sure that the sticks strike the drum head in the same area with each stroke.

Practice the following exercises first with the right hand alone, then with the left hand alone, and then with both hands alternating.

Let all the notes ring.

Exercise 1

Exercise 2

Exercise 3

Exercise 4

Moving From One Drum To Another

The technique in going from one drum to another is to anticipate the change of direction of the hands, thus when the right stick strikes the small drum and the next beats falls on the large drum with the left hand, the left hand should be on its way over to the large drum as soon as possible. This will help to eliminate dragging the tempo and make execution so much easier.

In playing tympani, the motion should be from hand to hand, preferably right, left, right, left. In many cases, this rule is violated for the convenience of sticking. However, **at all times,** the student should try to play from hand to hand.

Practice the following exercises keeping this principle in mind.

Exercise 7
In G & C
R L R L L R L R L R L R L R L R L R
L R L R L R L R L R L R L R L R L R L R R L
R R L R L R L R L R L R L R L R L R L
R L R L R L R L R L R L R L R L R L R
Exercise 8
In A & E
R L R R L R L R L R R L R L R L R L R R R L
L
R L R L R L R L R L R R L R L R L R L R L R L R L R L R L R L R L R
R L
R L R L R L R L R L R R L R L R L R R L R L R L R L R L R L
R L R L R L R L R R L R L R L R L R L R L R R L R R R L R R L R L R
Exercise 9
In C & F
R L R L R L R L R L R R R R L R R L R L R L L
R L R R L R L R L R L R R L R R L R L R R R L
L R L R L
R R L R R R L R R L R L R R L R L R L L R L R L R R L R L R R L R L R L R
R L R L R L R R L R L R L R L R L R L R L R L R L R L R L R L R R L R
L R L

The Roll

The purpose of the roll is to produce a sustained and even tone. The string player does this by continuing to draw the bow across the strings; the trumpeter does it by continuing to blow into the instrument. The tympanist must do it by rapid succession of strokes on the drum head.

When the proper stick and the proper technique are used, the roll can be executed so that it will sound like one continuous even tone, with none of the separate single beats being heard. The key to securing such a roll is the following (the student should keep this in mind while developing the roll):

1. The first stroke of the stick sets the head in vibration.

2. The object of every stroke after this is to sustain, to prolong the vibrations already set up. *The best quality roll will be obtained by striking two different spots in the same area of the head as in the open "V" picture on page 21.*

A series of strokes, no matter how rapid, will not produce an even and unbroken sound if the new vibrations are set up and destroyed with every stroke. Only a definite effort by the tympanist to keep the head in vibration and to sustain the vibrations already present, will produce a good roll.

The tympani roll is a single stroke roll. It should be practiced *using alternating strokes.*

The Speed Of The Roll

The speed of the roll will depend on two factors:

1. The tension of the head, *that is the pitch.* The higher the pitch, the greater the tension, therefore, the greater speed will be needed to keep the head in vibration. The lower the pitch, the less tension on the head, therefore, the speed of the roll will be less in order to keep the head in vibration.

2. The dynamics. The louder the dynamics the faster the roll. The softer the dynamics, the slower the roll.

Practice the exercise illustrating the roll. After the wrists are developed and you feel you have control, tune the drums to every note in the tympani range and take careful note of the different speeds necessary to keep the head in vibration.

Exercise 10

Different Types Of Rolls

1. The sustained roll:

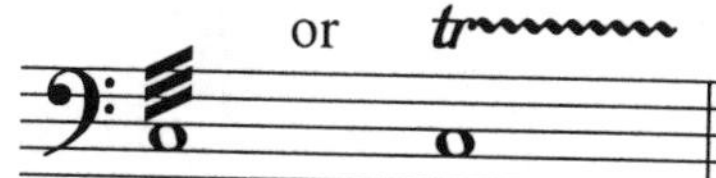

This is a continuous succession of strokes. Do not try to count the number of strokes in making a sustained roll.

2. The separated quarter roll:

If written out, this roll would look as follows (depending on the tempo), with the final note not audible.

*3. Two ways to play **measured rolls.***

First time, use a natural accent on the downbeat, alternate the pattern.

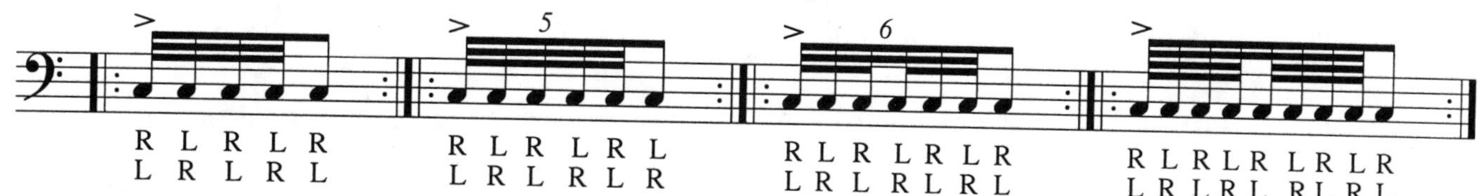

Second time, crescendo to the last note.

4. The tied eighth roll.

Use all of the above patterns with this exercise.

5. The short eighth roll or twirl.

This roll is always played as fast as possible.

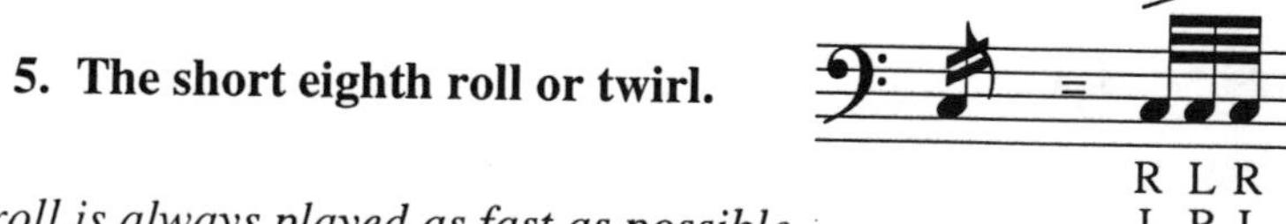

6. The short eighth roll in combination.

The roll should be attacked with the strong hand. In some cases where this is not practical, the other hand may be used. However, the strong hand should attack the roll at all other times. The student should try to make this a habit so that it comes automatically. Do not attack the roll by striking with both sticks at once.

Connecting The Roll From One Drum To Another

In rolling from drum to drum, the following procedure should be worked out in order not to break the roll.

1. From the small drum to the large drum.

Keep the right stick moving even as the left stick is about to strike the large drum.

2. From the large drum to the small drum.

Similarly, keep the left stick moving until the right stick is about to strike the small drum. This type of technique will require a great deal of practice to get real perfection. *Play the above using different tempos and dynamics.*

The Tied and Separated Roll

Most composers make no definite distinction between the tied and separated roll. When a roll is followed immediately by a single note, composers will not always connect the roll with the use of a tie or slur. ‿ Therefore, it is not always clear whether the roll is meant to be tied over to the beat or stopped slightly before the beat is struck.

From long experience, the author has found that most rolls are meant to be tied over to the beat that immediately follows.

A GOOD RULE TO REMEMBER, THEREFORE, IS TO TIE THE ROLL OVER TO THE BEAT FOLLOWING IT. AN EXCEPTION WOULD BE THE SHORT EIGHTH ROLL, WHICH SHOULD ALWAYS BE PLAYED AS WRITTEN.

For practice purposes, it is well for the students to acquaint themselves with the distinction between the tied and separated roll. Practice the exercises on the next two pages giving special attention to the difference between these two methods of playing the roll.

The tied roll is designated:

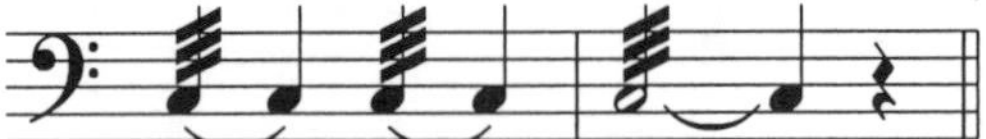

Here the roll is played right into the succeeding beat, **WITH THE BEAT ITSELF BEING STRUCK.**

The separated roll is designated:

Here the roll is stopped slightly before the succeeding beat is struck.

The Double-Stop Roll

To execute this type of roll, place the right stick on the small drum and the left stick on the large one and roll as if you were playing on one drum. *As these are half-note rolls, re-attack on the third beat.*

Practice Exercises 11 - 13 first as written, and then tie the rolls to the following note.

In A & D **Exercise 13**

♩ = 86

R L R R L R R L R L R L L R L R R R L
L L R L
L R L R L L R L R L R R L R R L R L R L L R L
L R L
R L L R R L R L R R R L R L R L R L
L R
L R L L R L L R L

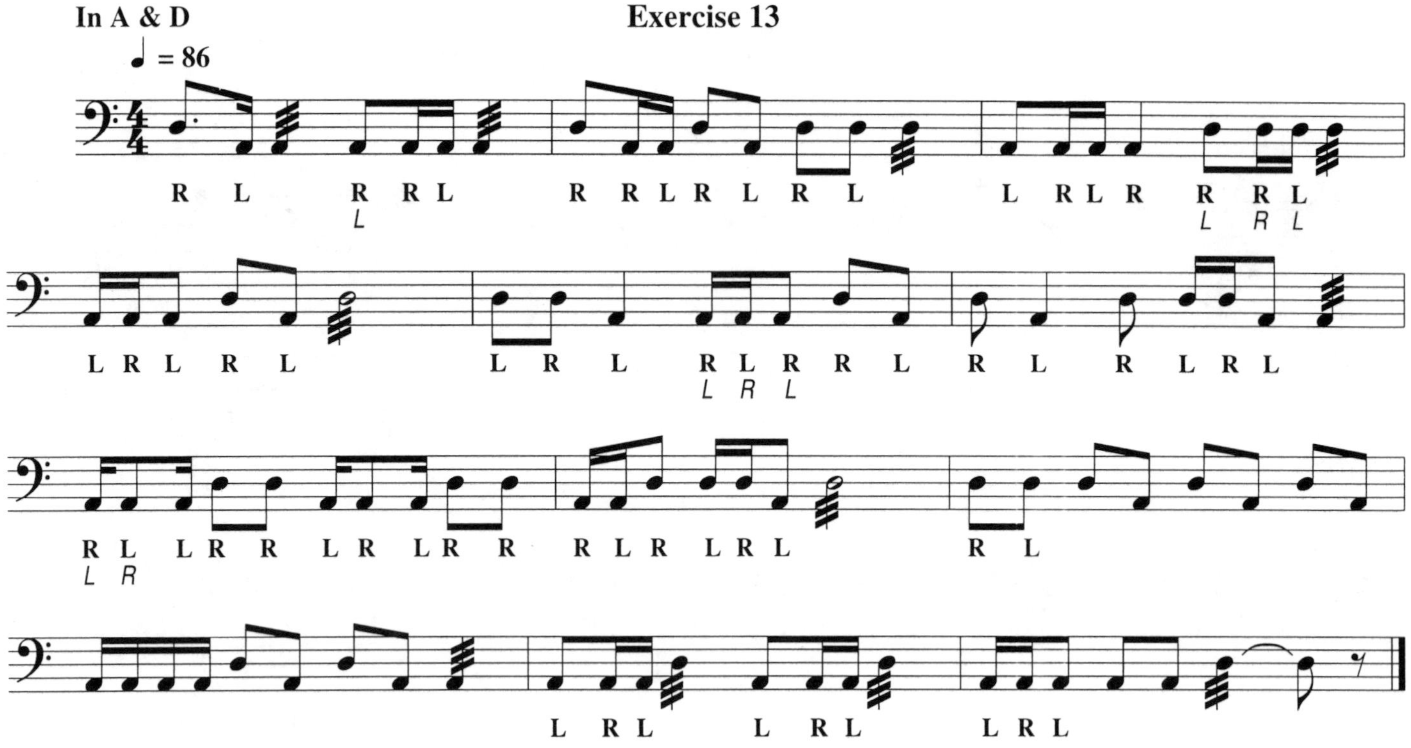

Practice Exercise 14 as written.

In G & C **Exercise 14**

♩ = 88

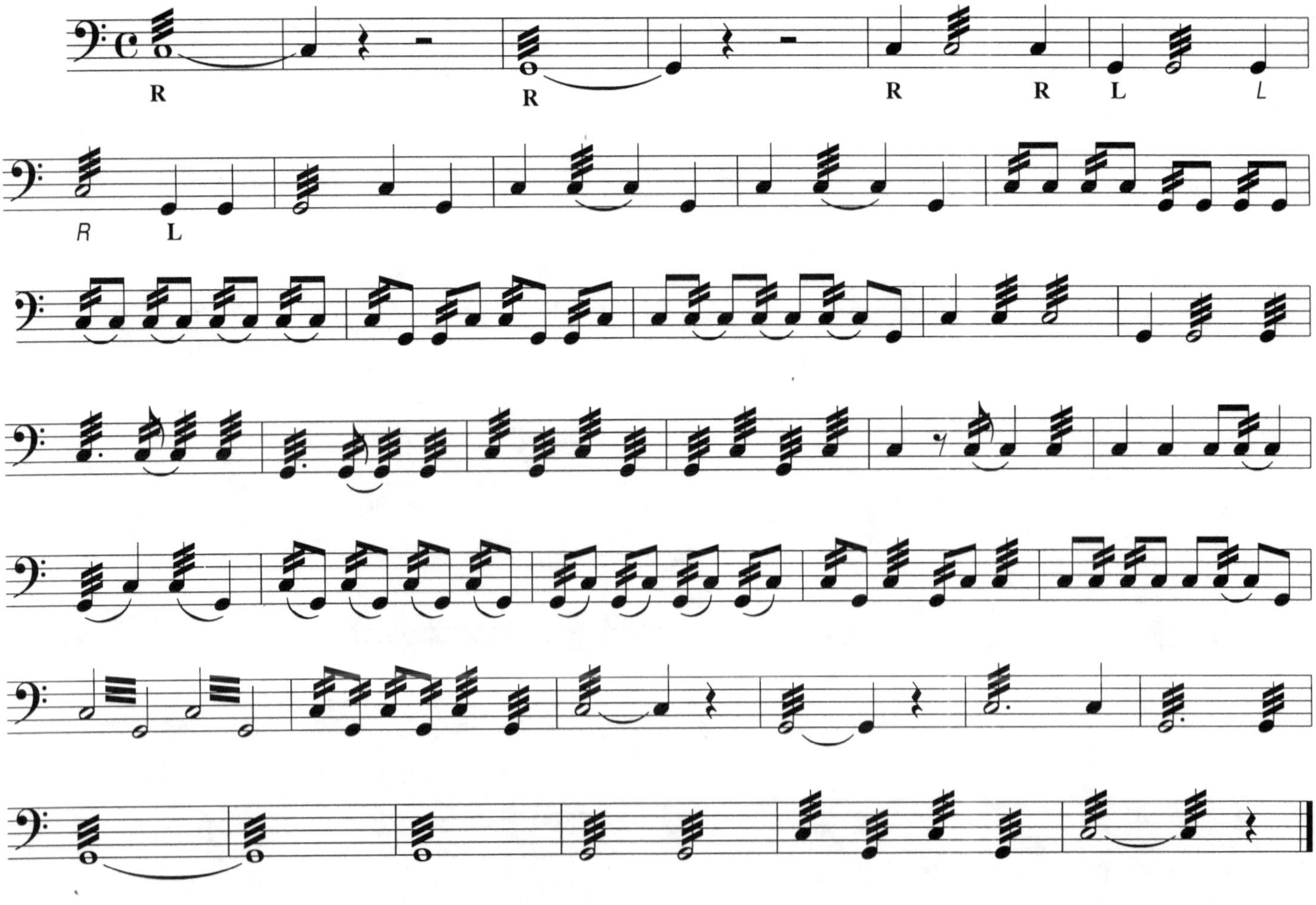
R R R R L L
R L

Muffling The Tympani

Proper muffling of the drum -- that is, stopping the vibrations of the head completely, is an important technical requirement.

In the first measure, the note is allowed to vibrate for the first two beats. The third beat is muffled, giving the half note it's proper time value. In the second measure, the eighth note is given it's proper time value by muffling on the eighth rest immediately following the beat.

However, when playing with an orchestra, listen to how they are phrasing and muffle accordingly.

There are two reasons for muffling; 1. to prevent the sustained tones of the drum from interfering with the succeeding tones or the succeeding harmonies of other instruments, and 2. to give the notes themselves their proper time values.

For example:

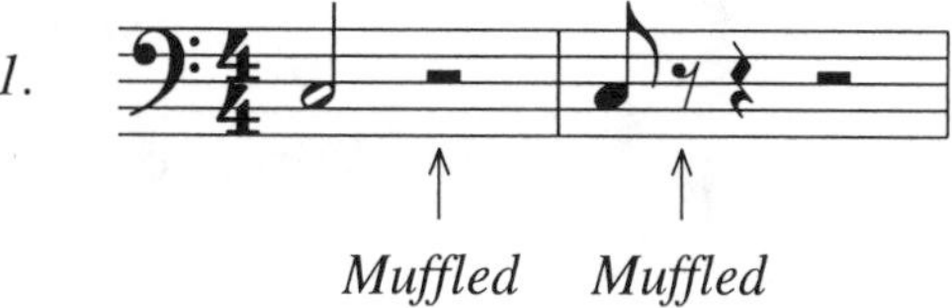

In this second example, each note is muffled precisely as the following note is struck.

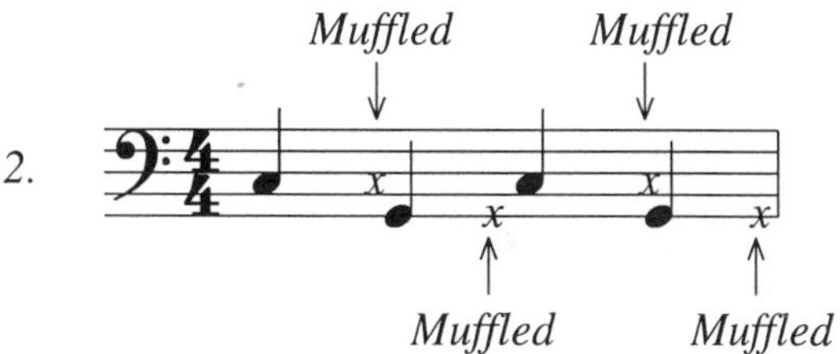

Method Of Muffling

Muffling should be done with the last three fingers of the hand, firmly but lightly against the head.

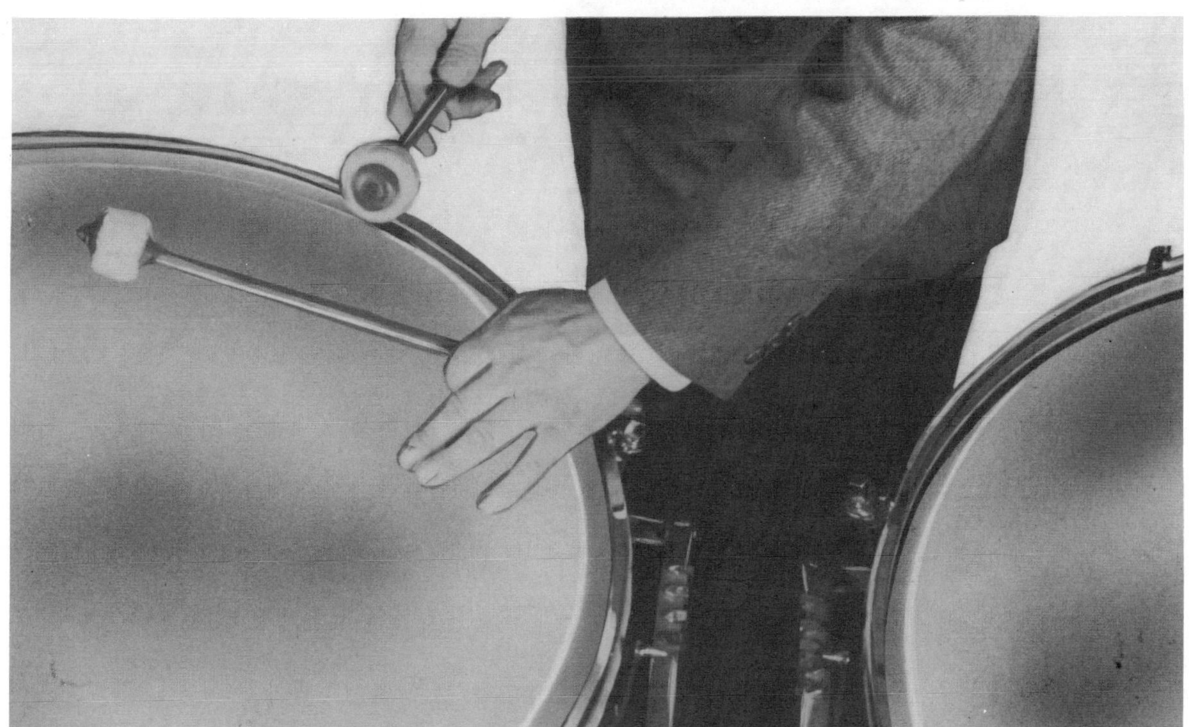

General Rules To Be Followed In Muffling

1. *Muffle the exact spot that is struck.*
2. When one single note is struck and is to be muffled, it is best to muffle with the hand that remains free.
3. In passages where a great deal of muffling is required, it is best to muffle with the hand that last strikes the drum.

Practice the following measures illustrating muffling from drum to drum.

Try this exercise by tuning the drums to different tones and noticing the amount of muffling needed for these tones.

Muffle on the rest following each note or set of notes.

The Loud Roll

In order to get the greatest amount of power from the tympani, it is necessary to change the position of the hands from that given in the chapter on "Holding the Sticks."

As the roll increases in volume beyond mf, the maximum distance from the hoop should be approached.

The following changes should be made in the positions of the hands:

1. The thumbs should be pointed upward.
2. The fourth finger is now in contact with the stick.
3. The sticks should be almost parallel to one another.
4. The player should step back very slightly. This position will give the greatest amount of freedom and enable the player to produce the maximum amount of volume.

In the loud roll, the forearms are used to assist the wrists and fingers.

Practice the roll from the softest degree to the loudest, returning to the same degree of softness. Note the change of position as given. Remember that as the roll decreases in volume, the player should resume the original position from which he started.

The Forte Piano *(fp)* Roll

There are two ways to play the standard fp roll.

1. This is a special type of roll characteristic of the tympani. To produce this roll properly, strike the drum with a forte attack. Allow the vibrations thus created to die away until it reaches the degree of softness desired. When this point is reached, start rolling again to maintain this required degree of softness. *Do not re-attack when beginning the roll.*

2. *Another way of playing the fp roll is by striking the drum at a forte level and then immediately continue rolling piano.*

The Extended Forte Piano Roll

There are places in the repertoire where the forte should be extended before dropping to piano. The amount of forte strokes may need to be determined by the player to fit in with the orchestration.

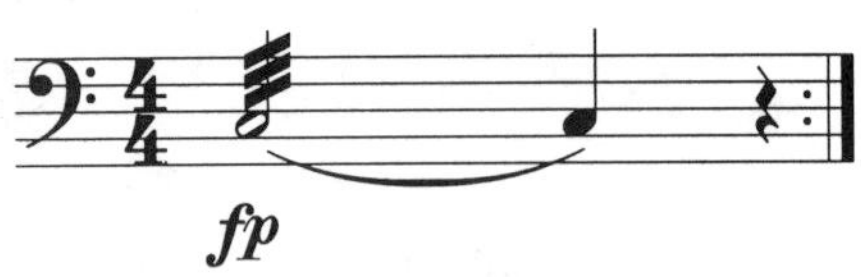

Practice starting the fp roll with both right and left-hand strokes.

The following exercise illustrates the forte piano and crescendo rolls.

Exercise 17

In G & C

Dynamic Control

Playing with the indicated dynamics is of the utmost importance to the tympanist. The ability of players to grade the dynamics to the greatest effect will largely determine their artistry on the instrument. In the extreme loud passages, the tone should never be forced so that the instrument no longer sounds like a tympani.

The degree of loudness and softness should be worked out by the student so that it will be most effective.

Work out the following exercises bearing this in mind.

Cross Sticking

A thorough knowledge of cross sticking is important to enable the player to execute fast passages between drums.

Cross sticking should not be overdone. The player should use this type of sticking with discretion. After a thorough understanding of this type of sticking, the player will soon learn to use it in its proper place.

How To Cross The Hands Properly

1. *The first four notes are played in the normal position.*
2. *Cross the right wrist over the left wrist. Strike the lower drum in the proper beating area for the fifth note.*
3. *The sixth note is played by the left hand with a "sweeping" motion while remaining in the crossing position.*
4. *The final two notes are played in the normal position.*

Practice the cross beats slowly at first, working for eveness in sound. After you feel secure in its execution, build the tempo up to a speed *as fast as possible while still articulating clearly.*

The Left-Hand Cross

This technique is done in the same manner as the right-hand cross with the exception that *the movements are reversed.*

Proper execution of the cross-sticking technique will insure that neither the hands nor the sticks collide.

Study all the different types of cross stickings below. Practice each one separately until mastered.

In A & D

Cross Sticking Examples
(In Sixteenths)

No.1
R L R L⊗R L R L

No.2
R L⊗R L R L⊗R L

No.3
R L R⊗L R L R⊗L

No.4
L R L⊗R L R L⊗R

No.5
L R L⊗R L R L⊗R L R L R⊗L R L R
R⊗L R L R⊗L R L R L⊗R L R L⊗R L

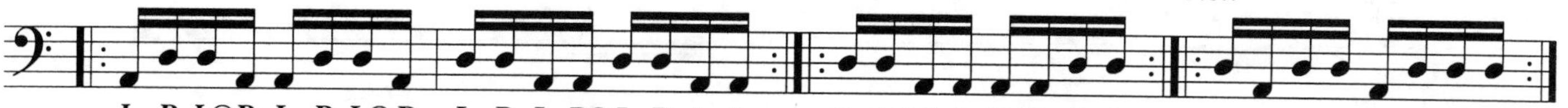

No.6
R L⊗R L R L R L

No.7
R L R L⊗R L R L

No.8
R L⊗R L R L

No.9 
R L⊗R L R L R L⊗R L R L⊗R L R L R L⊗R L R L R⊗L R L

No.10
L R L⊗R L R

No.11 
L R L⊗R L R L R L⊗R L R L R L⊗R L R L⊗R L R L⊗R L R L⊗R

No.12
R L R⊗L R⊗L R L

No.13
L R L R⊗L R L R

Practice Exercise 20 illustrating cross sticking in quarters, eights, and sixteenths. In the event difficulties are encountered, the student should refer back to the Cross Sticking Examples.

Cross Sticking In Triple Time

The Staccato Stroke

It is often necessary to produce a clear, concise stroke *for clarity of articulation.* It is important to develop the staccato stroke in order to properly attain this sound.

How To Develop The Staccato Stroke

The student should first refer to the chapter on Holding The Sticks. Review this position and take special note of the thumb and first 3 fingers. By exerting different pressures with these fingers on the stick, it will be noted that different sounds can be produced on the tympani.

To achieve the Ultra-Staccato stroke, follow the procedure below:

1. *Place the sticks approximately 2 1/2 inches from the rim.*
2. *Use a short, choppy stroke.*
3. *First squeeze, then relax the fingers after playing quarter or eighth notes. There will not be time to relax the fingers when playing sixteenth notes.*
4. *This technique is good for playing up to a single forte. Use the "thumb on top" grip explained on page 33 for fortissimo staccato strokes.*

Practice the following exercises making a special effort for each phrase to be clearly heard by exerting the correct amount of pressure between the thumb and first 3 fingers.

In A & D **Exercise 22**

♩ = 100

R L R L

Ⓧ

R

R R L R L R R L R L R L R L R L R L R L R L R L
L

R L R L R L R L R L R L R L Ⓧ

R L RL R L R LR L R L R L R R L Ⓧ R L R R L R L Ⓧ R
L R L R L

R L R L R R L R L Ⓧ R R L R Ⓧ L R L R L R L R Ⓧ L R L R Ⓧ L R L
L L R L

R L R L R L R R L R R L R

In B♭ & E♭

Exercise 23

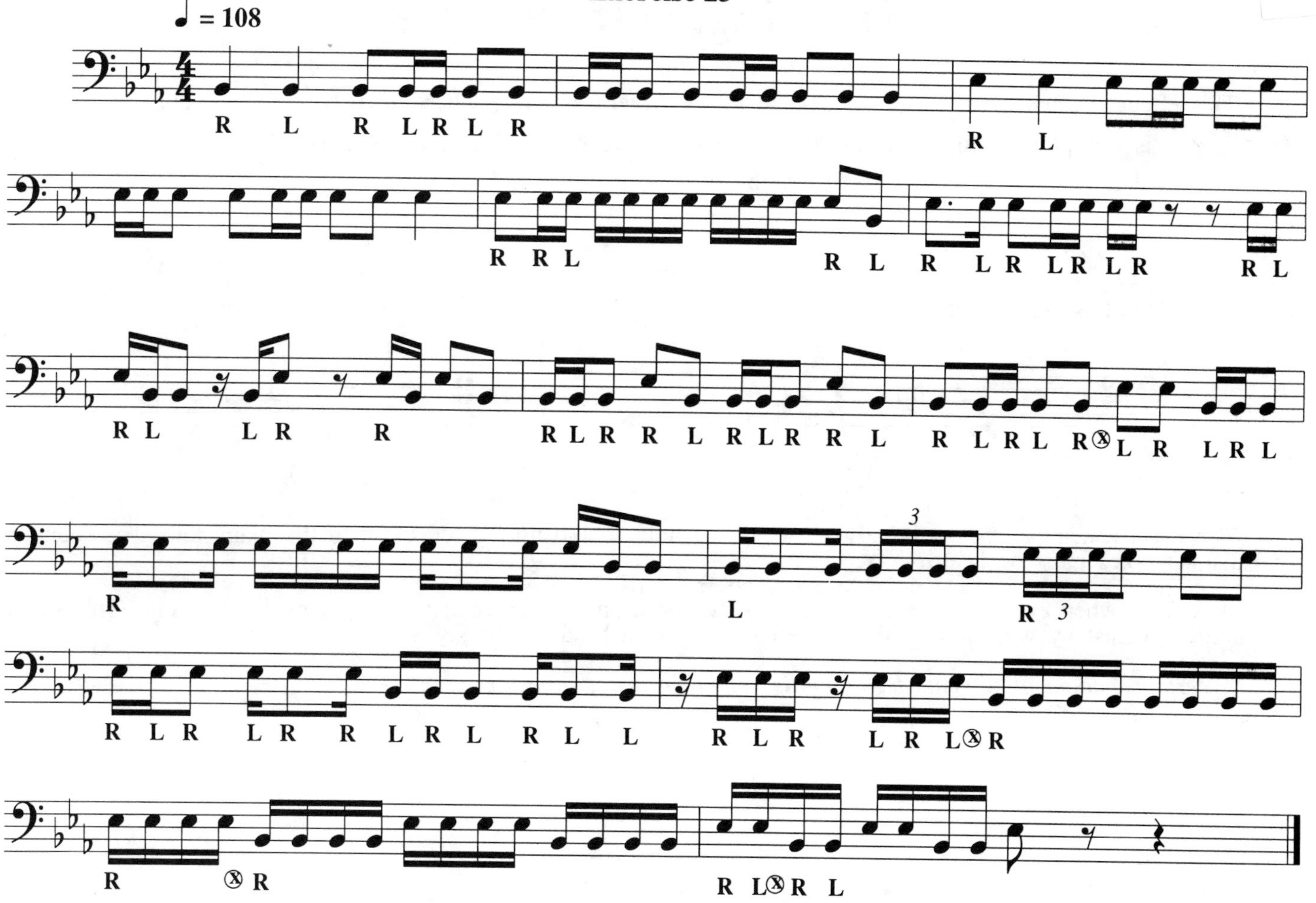

♩ = 108

R L R L R L R

R L

R R L R L R L R L R L R L R L R L

R L L R R R L R R L R L R R L R L R R L R L R L R L R L

R L R 3

R L R L R R L R L R L L R L R L R L R

R R R L R L

Staccato In The Low Register Of The Tympani

The following exercise will serve to illustrate the difficulty of producing the staccato in the lower tones. Practice this exercise making a special effort to make the notes clearly heard. *Be sure to use the 28" and 25" tympani for this exercise and also play it with the drums tuned to low F and B♭.*

Exercise 24

In G & C

The Single Grace Note

This effect is often used, and in its several forms is very effective when properly executed. The single grace note is ***not*** played similar to the "flam" on the snare drum. The small (grace) note is played just before the beat; the large note is played directly on the beat.

What is written this way:

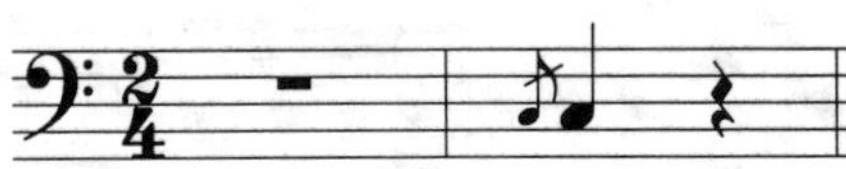

Is played as though written:

The execution must not be too "tight"; the grace note should not be too close to the main note. The sound of two distinct notes must be heard.

It is easy, when executing a grace note, to stifle the drum and prevent it from giving its true tone. This should be guarded against by withdrawing the stick from the drum head as quickly as possible.

A certain amount of staccato technique is helpful in articulating grace notes.

The Double Grace Note

Written:

It is played as though written:

Three distinct sounds must be heard. The most effective method (for right-hand players) is right-left-right so that the stronger right hand naturally plays the downbeat.

No grace-note begins with an attack or accent unless indicated.

The Triple Grace Note

Here the three small notes preceding the main note have the effect of a triplet.

Written:

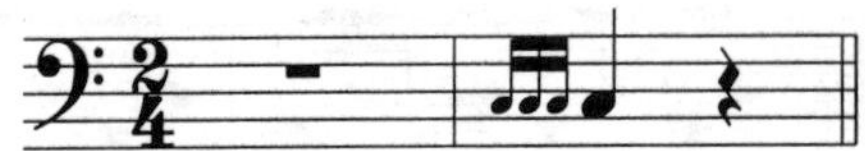

It is played as though written:

The Quadruple Grace Note

This grace note pattern is not as common as the previous three in tympani music.

Played:

When it occurs, it is most often played in one of the two ways indicated below, practice at all dynamic levels.

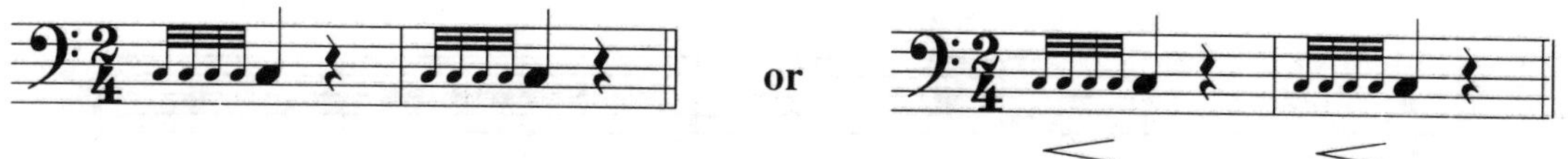

Practice the following exercise on grace notes taking great care not to play them too closely. Grace notes are most effective when played slowly. Do not attempt to play the exercise too rapidly.

At first, play Exercise 25 in 8 (♪ = 86). Then repeat it in a Moderato tempo. The first two measures of the last line are the most difficult and may determine how fast to take the Moderato tempo.

In G & D

***Moderato* ♩ = 64**

Counting Rests

The ability to count accurately the number of measures rest, no matter how numerous, is one of the most important requisites in Tympani playing.

This ability can be developed only by the most careful concentration and closest attention to the rhythmical structure of the music being played. Conductors cannot always give an entrance cue to the tympanist, and for this reason the player must be absolutely certain and sure just when he must "set in."

Let us look first at several simpler types of rhythm in which rests occur;

Here there are two beats in a measure, that is, the rhythm is "1, 2, 1, 2, . . . " Then when we come to the three measures rests we will count as follows:

"*1*, 2, *2*, 2, *3*, 2"—and then play.

Notice how the first beat of each measure is used to indicate the numbers of measures rest counted. This can of course be continued as long as necessary, according to the number of measures rest in question.

Example (2) has four beats to a measure; the rhythm is then "1—2—3—4, 1—2—3—4, . . . " Therefore in counting the 4 measures rest in example 2 we say "*1*—2—3—4, *2*—3—3—4, *3*—2—3—4, *4*—2—3—4," and come in on the first beat of the next measure as indicated.

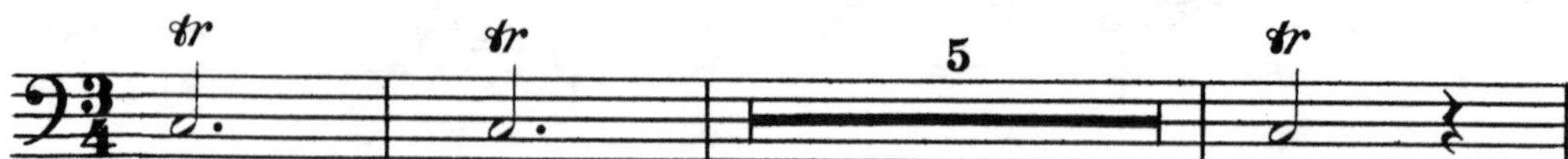

In example 3 the five measures rest is counted:
"*1*—2—3, *2*—2—3, *3*—2—3, *4*—2—3, *5*—2—3."

These examples should suffice to make clear the general system used in counting measures rest, and the student will easily find applications of this system to many other rhythmical patterns.

In many cases where there are a great many measures rest for the tympanist they are divided into groups, often separated by "cues" played by other instruments, giving the tympanist an opportunity to check his position. His ability to use these cues will depend largely upon his keenness in detecting them in the orchestra.

Counting rests and tuning the drums at the same time is not an easy trick, and can be developed only through constant practice. The player will find some difficulty in continuing to count accurately while trying to bring the drum to some required pitch at the same time. The key to the matter lies in becoming so adept at counting rests that it becomes an automatic process, and will go on by itself while the player pays attention to tuning.

If the tympanist does lose his place he may be able to find it again by his "cues." If none are provided on his music in a difficult section he will do well to enter his own.

The knack of counting and tuning cannot be acquired overnight. Regular and consistent practice is the only way to achieve this important skill.

In the orchestra, the player should so place himself that no matter how many drums surround him he will be able to see the conductor at all times—even when bending over his drums at any extreme angle.

In the preceding pages the fundamentals of Tympani playing have been developed. These fundamentals are important for a real understanding of the instrument.

The following exercises will serve to give the student a more thorough knowledge of the technical resources of the instrument.

In working out these exercises, if the student should run across difficulties he may always refer back to the fundamentals for assistance.

In many cases the author's hammering has been notated; other places have been left blank for the student to use his own.

Hammering is often the case of personal choice provided that the player has a thorough background in the fundamentals.

Do not work only for speed. The important things to work for are:
Clarity.
Precision.
Tempo.
Tone.

At all times exercise good musical taste in your playing.

SECTION TWO

Exercises For The Development Of Technique On Two Drums

In A♭ & E♭

Exercise 28

Tempo di polonaise ♩ = 88

f *marcato*

ff

p

f

* See page 31 for muffling technique.

In B♭ & F

Exercise 29

Not too fast ♩. = 72

f

f > *mf*

fp < *f*

p

ff

In G & D

Exercise 30

Allegretto ♩. = 88

f

 9/2/10

In B & E

Exercise 31

Tempo di marcia ♩ = 80

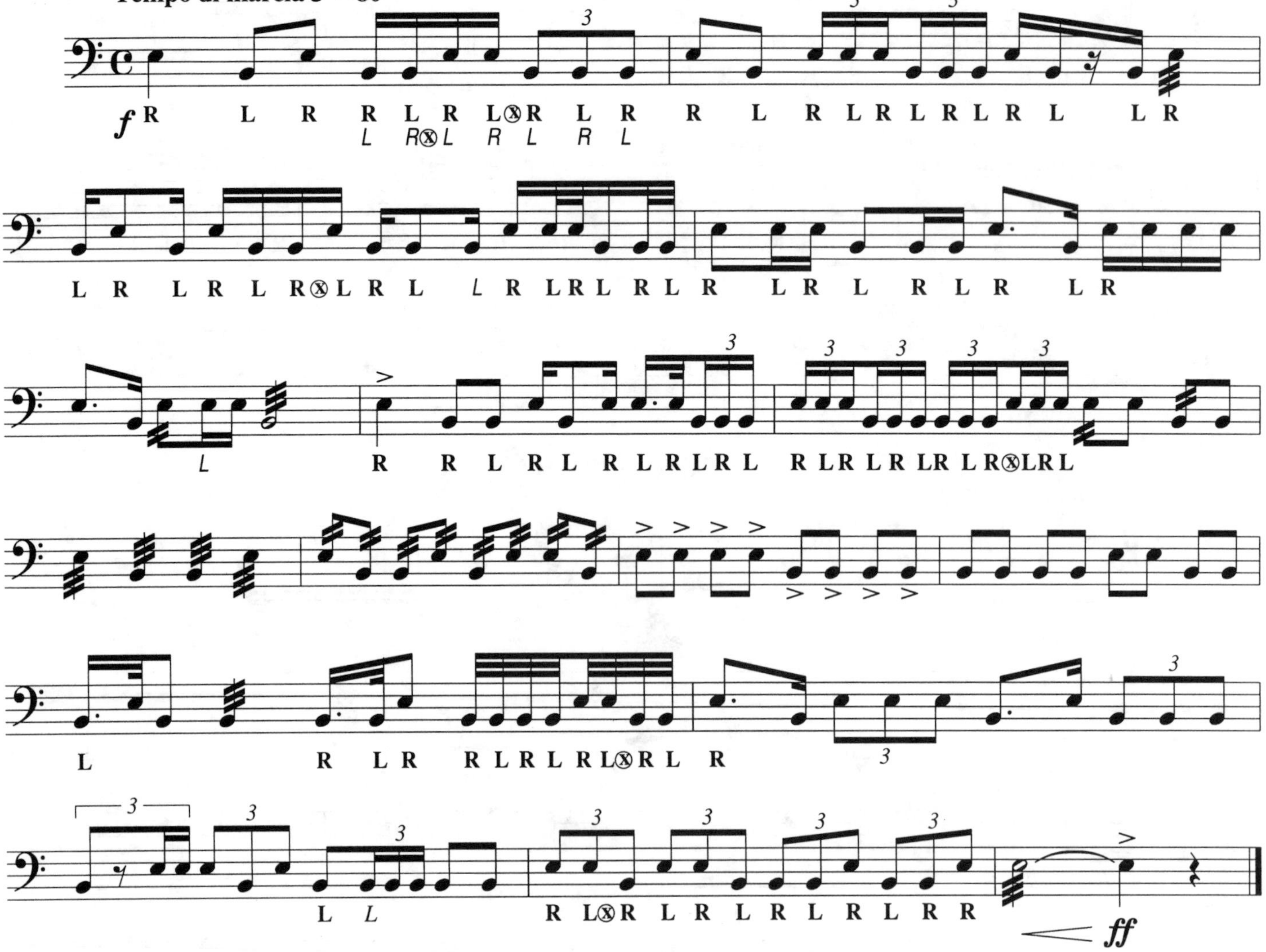
f
ff

In B♭ & F

Exercise 32

Allegro giocoso ♩ = 84

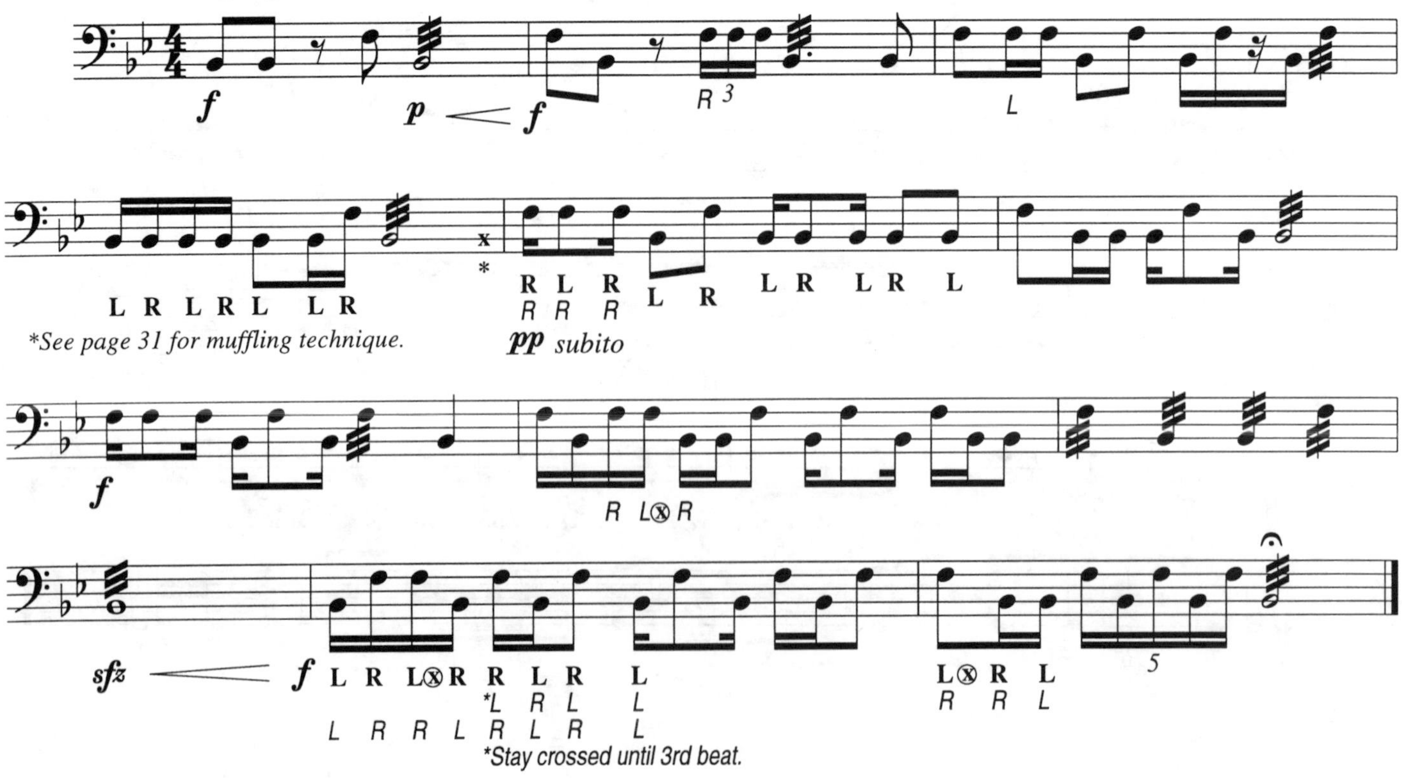
f
p
f
*See page 31 for muffling technique.
pp subito
f
sfz
f
*Stay crossed until 3rd beat.

In C & F

Exercise 33

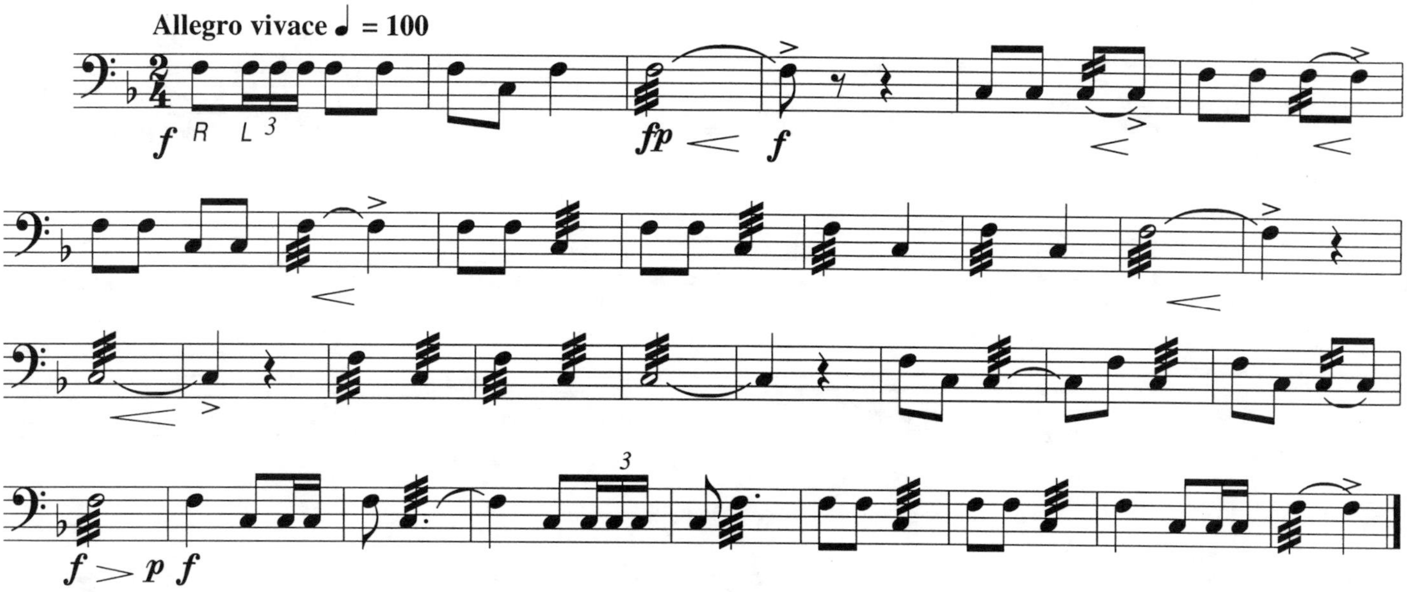

Allegro vivace ♩ = 100

f R L 3 *fp* *f*

f > *p* *f*

In A & E

Exercise 34

♩ = 88

f R L R L R L R L R L R L R L R L R L R L R

R R R L R L R L R L R L R L R L L R

R L R L R L
L R L L R L
R R L
p L R L R LR LR L 3

R L⊗R L R L R L⊗R L R L R L⊗R L R L⊗R L R R L R L R R L R L
cresc. poco a poco - - - - - - - - - - - - - - -

f *ff* L R L R L R L⊗R L R
R L

L R L R L R L R L⊗R L R L R R L R R L R L R L L R L R R L R L R L

R L R L⊗R L R L R L⊗R L R R L R L R L R L R R L R L R L R L R L R L

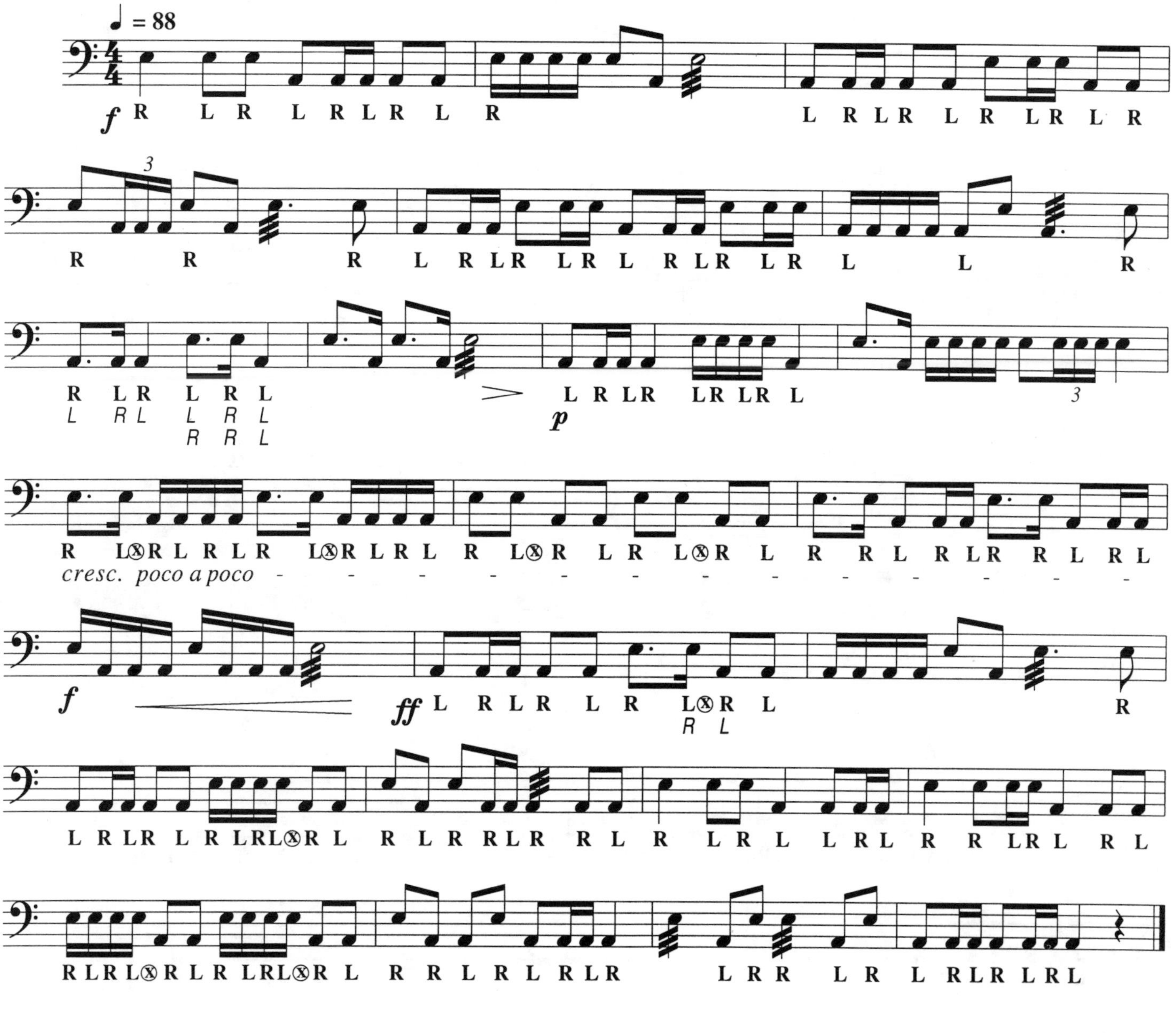

In F & B♭
Exercise 35
𝅗𝅥 = 72
In A♭ & E♭
Exercise 36
Allegro preciso
accel.
In G & C
Exercise 37
Andante maestoso
cresc.

In A♭ & E♭
Exercise 38
Tempo di valse
cresc.
If played as a tremolo.
Exercise 39
In C & F
♩ = 72
Exercise 40
In F & B♭
Adagio ♩ = 66
rit.

In A♭ & E♭

Exercise 41

♩. = 76

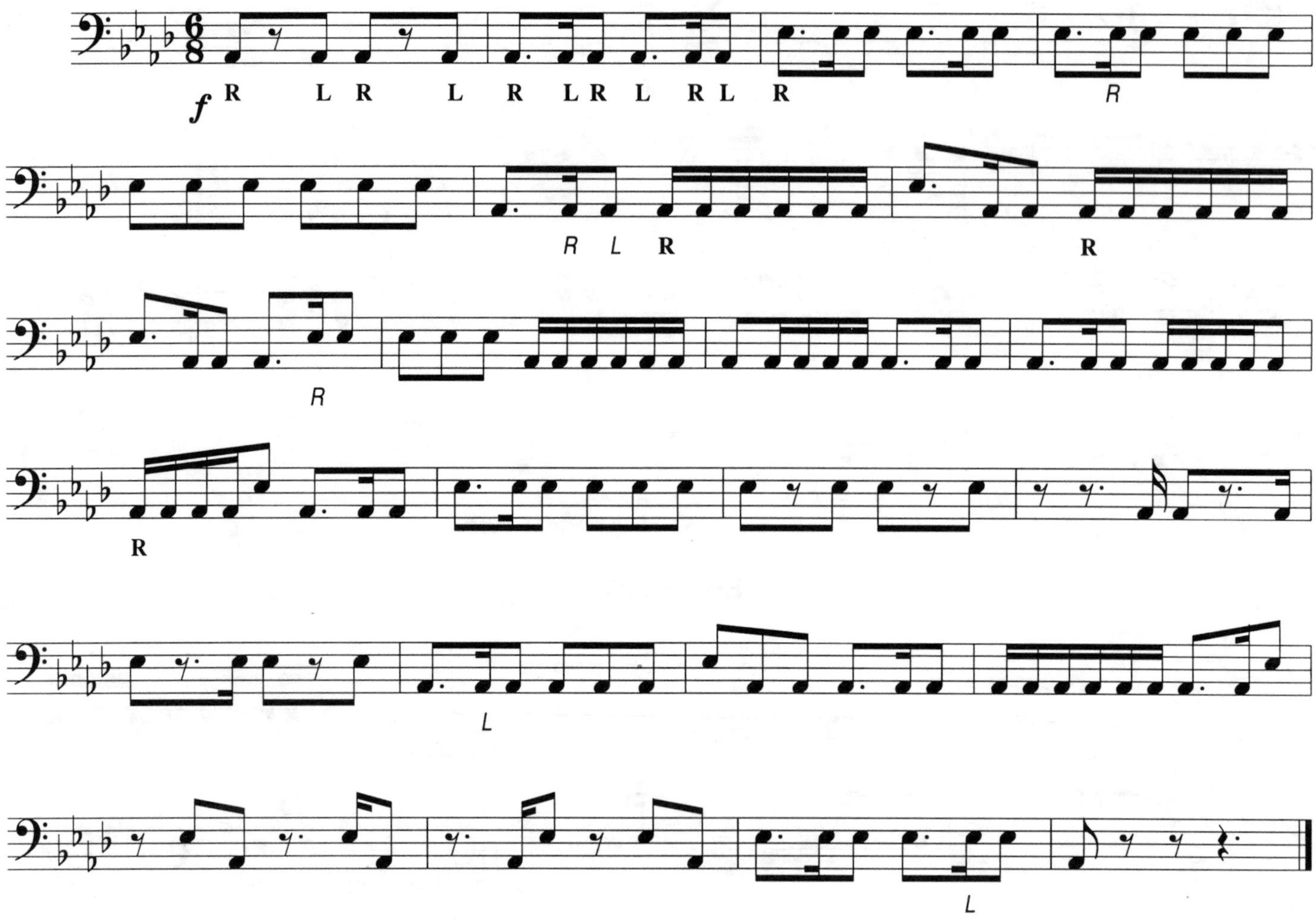

f
R L R L R L R L R L R
R
R L R
R
R
R
L
L

In A♭ & E♭

Exercise 42

Tempo di marcia ♩ = 88

f
mp
cresc. - - - - - -
f
fp
ff
R LR⊗LR⊗LR L
R
tutta forza

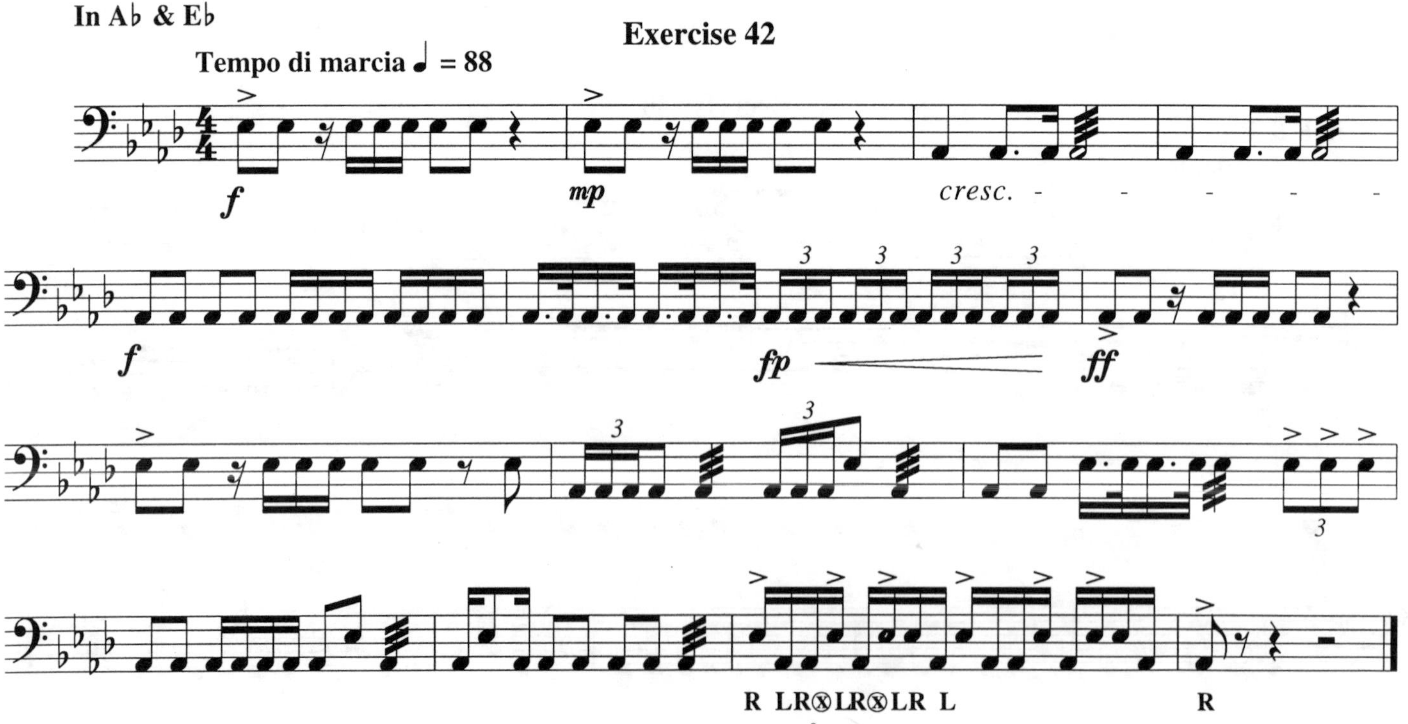

In A & D

Exercise 43

In A♭ & D♭
Exercise 45
Allegro ♩ = 92
In B & E
Exercise 46
Andante preciso 𝅗𝅥 = 76
cresc.

In B♭ & E♭
Exercise 47
𝅗𝅥 = 80
f
In A & E
Exercise 48
♩. = 76
f
p cresc.
f
ff
In B & E
Exercise 49
♩ = 90
f
fp
f

Exercise 50

* *Begin with right hand and alternate with cross sticking, except as noted.*

Exercise 51

Where measure indicates 3/4, count three beats to the measure.
Where measure indicates 6/8, count two beats to the measure.

In A & E

In C & F

Exercise 52

In B♭ & E♭
Exercise 53
Slow march ♩ = 66
f
R L⊗R L R L R L⊗R
L R L R L R R L R
R L R L R L R L R L R L
R L⊗R L
LRL⊗R L RLR⊗LR L R LRL RL
R L⊗R L R L⊗R L R⊗LR L R⊗LR L RL⊗R L R L⊗R L
R L R L R⊗LR L⊗R L R L
fp
R L R L⊗R L
cresc.
ff
In A & D
Exercise 54
♩ = 80
f
L
R R
R
L
♪ = ♪
L
L R L R R L R L R
R
L⊗
R
R R R L R L L
R
L R L L
R R

In C & F
Exercise 55
Allegro ♩ = 108
cresc.
rit.
In B♭ & E♭
Exercise 56
♩ = 76
p subito
cresc.

In F & C
Exercise 57
♩ = 92
To G & D
cresc.
To C & A
A to F
In G & D
Exercise 58
𝅗𝅥 = 64
To B♭ & F
cresc.
F to E♭
To Low F & C

SECTION THREE

Three And Four Drum Technique

The two middle drums should be directly in front of the player with the lowest drum on the extreme left. This will form a small semi-circle.

With four drums, the fourth drum should be placed so that the player is in the exact center within easy reach of every drum.

In some cases, with modern scores, a fifth drum has to be added. The drums should then be placed in as small a semi-circle as possible so that the player is within easy reach of each drum. Care should be taken so that in going from one drum to another, the screws or the counter hoops of the drums are not struck.

Technique Of Three And More Drums

Cross sticking to extreme drums should be avoided. In some rare cases, this might have to be done. Two strokes with one hand on adjacent drums is often necessary.

Three Drum Examples

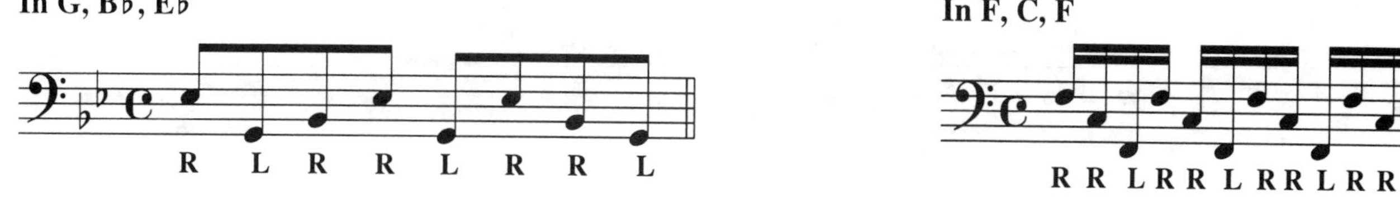

Four Drum Examples

Three Drum Exercises

In G, B♭, D

Exercise 59

* See page 31 for muffling technique.

In G, C, E
Exercise 63
Lento ♩. = 56
In A, D, F
Exercise 64
Presto 𝅘𝅥𝅯 = 160

In G, C, E
Exercise 65
Moderato ♩. = 84
accel.
In F, C, E
Exercise 66
Allegro vivace ♩ = 96
In F, B♭, F
Exercise 67
Allegro moderato ♩ = 88

In G, C, D
Exercise 68
Not too fast ♩ = 76
mf
In F♯, B, E
Exercise 69
Slowly ♩ = 69
f
fp
f
ff
mf
accel. e. cresc.
f
ff
fff

Four Drum Exercises

In G, C, E♭, F

Exercise 72

Technique With The Pedal Tympani

The versatile use of the pedal tympani is the ultimate achievement in the technical mastery of the tympani.

To achieve the highest results the ear must be perfectly developed. Since the calf tympani head is so unstable on account of atmospheric conditions, a great deal depends on the players themselves in determining the accuracy of the pitch.

Before beginning the technical studies for pedal tympani, refer to the chapter on tuning with the pedal tympani. Make sure the pedal is set so the complete range is available on each drum.

It will be relatively simple to play the following exercises if the student will strike the drum first with the pedal in a released position and then slide up to the desired note.

After the technique with the pedal has been developed, the use of muffling in stopping one tone from sliding into another may be exercised freely.

The Glissando (Gliss)

The glissando is done by striking the drum with the pedal released and sliding up to the note desired. This may also be done in reverse by tuning to the highest note, striking the drum and releasing the pedal, sliding downward to the desired note. The most effective form of glissando, however, is upward.

L = Large Drum
S = Small Drum

Exercises For Pedal Tympani

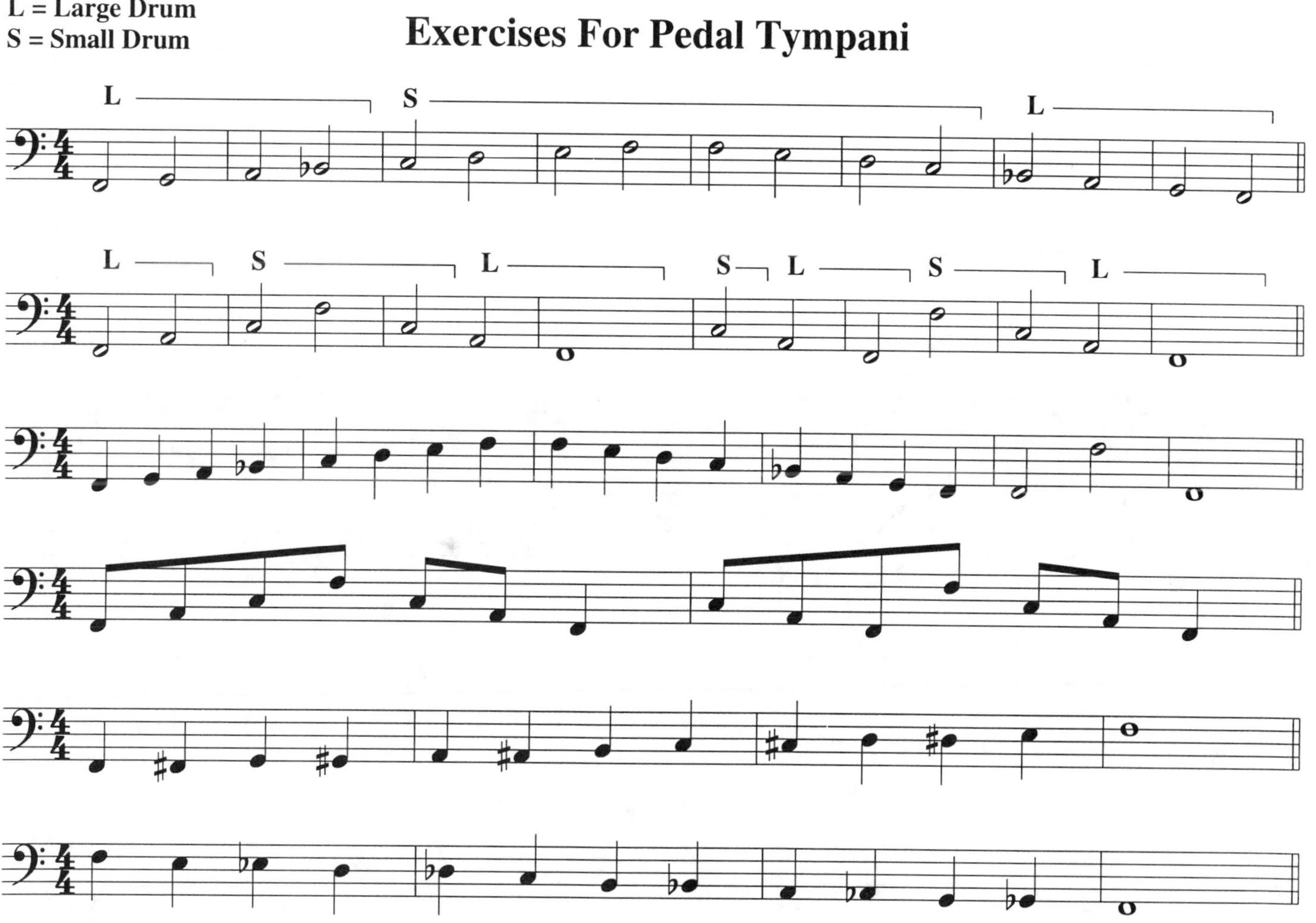

The Glissando

Melodies For The Pedal Tympani

America

Samuel F. Smith
mf
My Old Kentucky Home
Andante
Stephen C. Foster
mf
March from "Aida"
Moderato
G. Verdi
f

5 Drum Study

For most practical cases, the use of 4 mechanical tympani will be sufficient to solve most of the technical problems in the modern repertoire. There are cases, however, where the player will find it necessary to employ 5 tympani. The exercise given below will serve to illustrate the use of the fifth drum. The player should be careful to arrange the drums so each one is within convenient striking range.

*SECTION FOUR; Repertoire for Tympani

Symphony No. 101

by FRANZ JOSEPH HAYDN

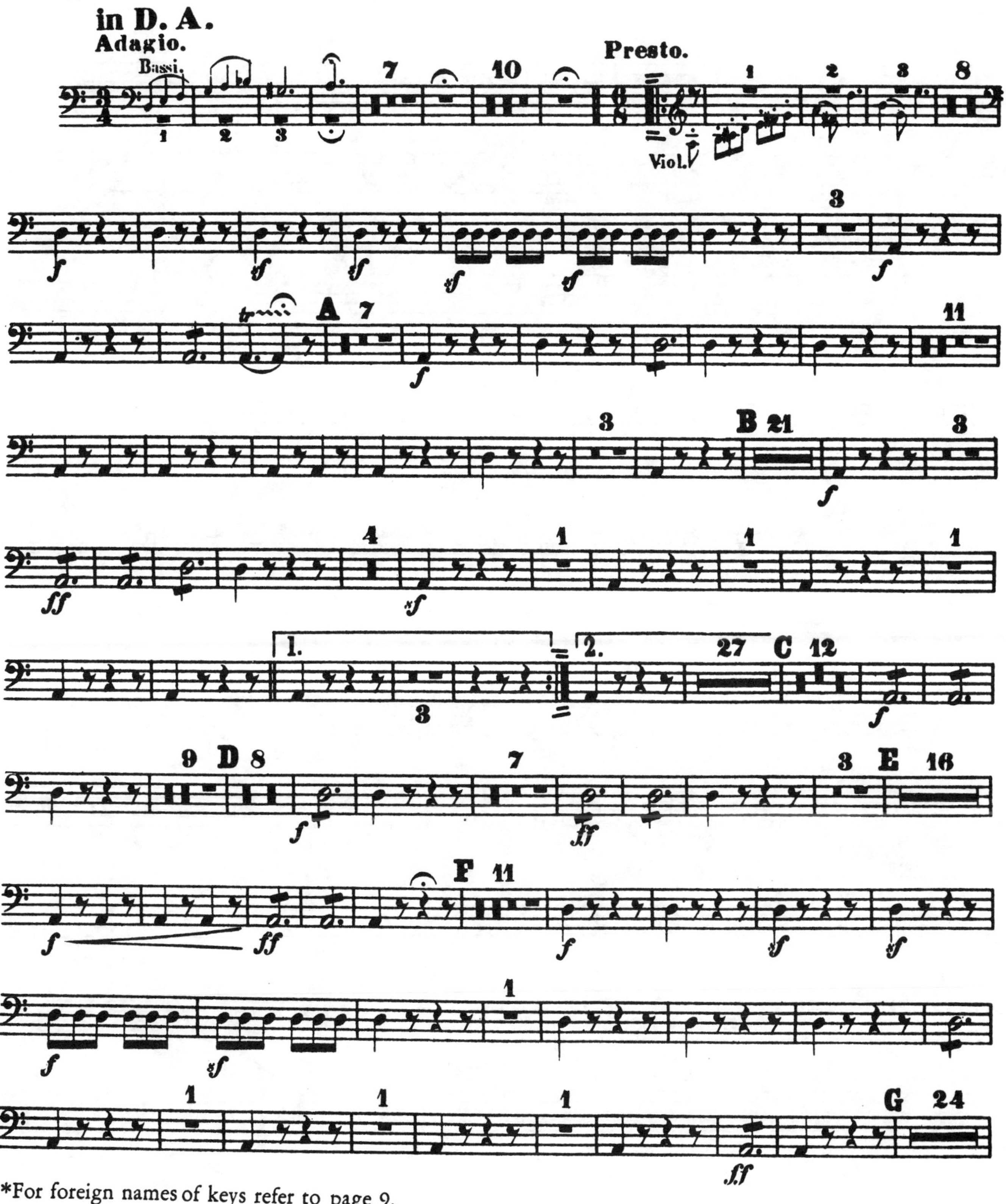

*For foreign names of keys refer to page 9.

H
I
in D.G.
Andante.
Viol. I.
Viol. II.
K
Fl. I.
Minore.
L
Maggiore.
M
N
O
G. P.
P
Fl. I.
Q
in D. A.
MENUETTO.
Allegretto.

Trio.
in D. A.
FINALE.
Vivace.
Viol. I.
Men. D. C.
Minore.
Maggiore.
Viol. I.

Symphony No. 5

by LUDWIG VAN BEETHOVEN, op. 67

Tympani in C & G

Andante con moto. (♪ = 92)
Viol. I
Holz.
A
ff sempre
Viol. I
Holz.
B
Viol. I
C
Cor.
D
dim.
Holz.
cresc.
E
Più moto. (♪ = 116)
Viol. I
Tempo I.
Viola
Allegro.
(𝅗𝅥. = 96)
poco ritard.
a tempo
poco rit.
a tempo
poco rit.
a tempo
Bassi
Viol. I
cresc.
Viol. II
poco rit.
a tempo
poco rit.
a tempo
Fag. Vcl.
Viol. I
sempre pp

cresc.
attacca
Allegro. (𝅗𝅥 = 84)
ff
Bassi
Tromb.
f
B
più f
A
C
Viol. II
D
E
ff sempre
Tempo I. (𝅗𝅥. = 96)
Fl.
pp
cresc.
Allegro. (𝅗𝅥 = 84)

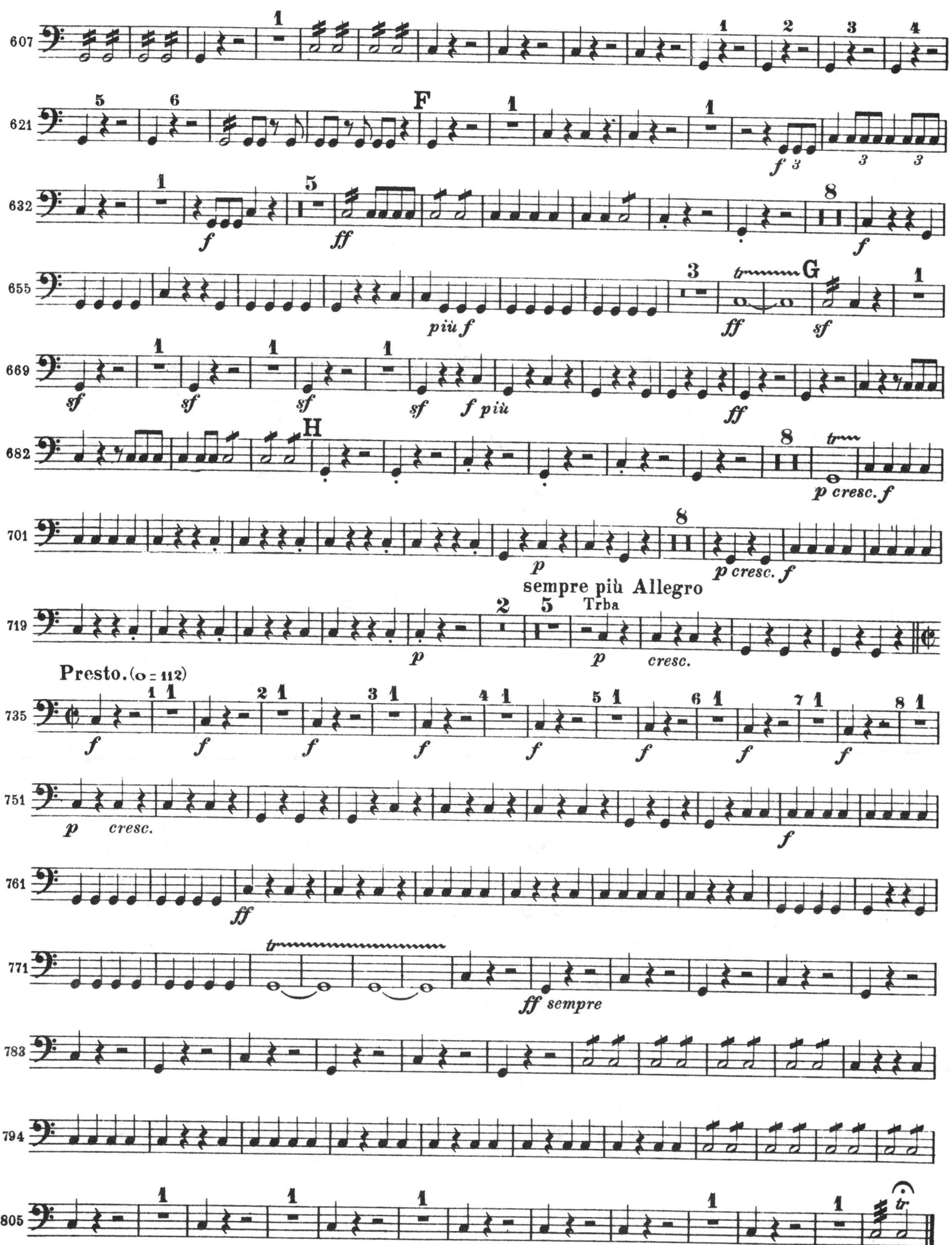
F
più f
G
H
p cresc. f
sempre più Allegro
Trba
cresc.
Presto. (o = 112)
ff sempre

Symphony No. 7

by LUDWIG VAN BEETHOVEN, op. 92

15
2
2
22
poco cresc.
piu cresc.
Allegretto 𝅗𝅥 = 76
in
A. E.
74
dimin.
3
37
6
24
cresc.
29
19
26
Presto 𝅗𝅥. = 132
in
F. A.
14
33
27
4
19
2
Assai meno presto
32
26
13

Presto
14
sempre p
33
27
19
Assai meno presto
26
32
13
CODA
Assai meno presto
Allegro con brio
= 72
in
A.E.
p cresc. poco a poco
10

9
1.
2.
8
11
4
8
pp
ff
f
P cresc. poco a poco
1 2 3 4 5 6 7 8 9 10 11 12
12
2
13
5
3
7
6
sempre piu f ff
fff
p
cresc.

Symphony No. 9

by LUDWIG VAN BEETHOVEN, op. 125

Allegro ma non troppo, un poco maestoso ♩= 88

K
L
M
N
O
P
Q
R
cresc.
dim.
a tempo
ritard.

p
cresc.
f
piu f
S
ff
sempre ff
tr
sf
in
Molto vivace
Solo
G.P.
A
B
C
D
Ritmo di tre battute.
Ritmo di quattro battute.
E
dim.
F
pp
cresc.
piu cresc.
G
H
I
K
stringendo il tempo
Presto
L
M
poco ritard.
Molto vivace
Solo
N
O
P

Ritmo di tre battute.
Solo
G.P.
dim.
Ritmo di quattro battute.
pp
cresc.
piu cresc.
piu f
ff
Coda
stringendo il tempo
cresc.
Presto
G.P.
Adagio molto e cantabile
Andante moderato
Tempo I
Solo
in
* B. F.
Andante moderato
Adagio
Lo stesso tempo
sempre p
cresc.
dim.
piu p
Solo
sempre pp

*(B♭) see page 9.

in
D.A.
Presto = 96
Allegro ma non troppo = 88
Tempo I
poco Adagio
ritard.
Vivace
Tempo I
Adagio cantabile
Tempo I
Allegro assai
Tempo I
Allegro assai = 80
A
B
C
poco
riten.
poco Adagio
Tempo I
Solo
Presto
Recit.
colla voce
Allegro assai
ad lib.
D
sempre
E
dim.
F
G
molto ten.
Allegro assai = 84
H
I
K
L
Viol. I
M

Andante maestoso
Adagio ma non troppo, ma divoto
𝅗𝅥 = 60
𝅗𝅥. = 84
Allegro energico, sempre ben marcato
Allegro ma non tanto 𝅗𝅥 = 120
poco Adagio
Tempo I
poco Adagio
Poco Allegro, stringendo il tempo
Prestissimo 𝅗𝅥 = 132
Maestoso 𝅘𝅥 = 60
Prestissimo
sempre ff

Symphony No. 4

by FELIX MENDELSSOHN-BARTHOLDY, op 90

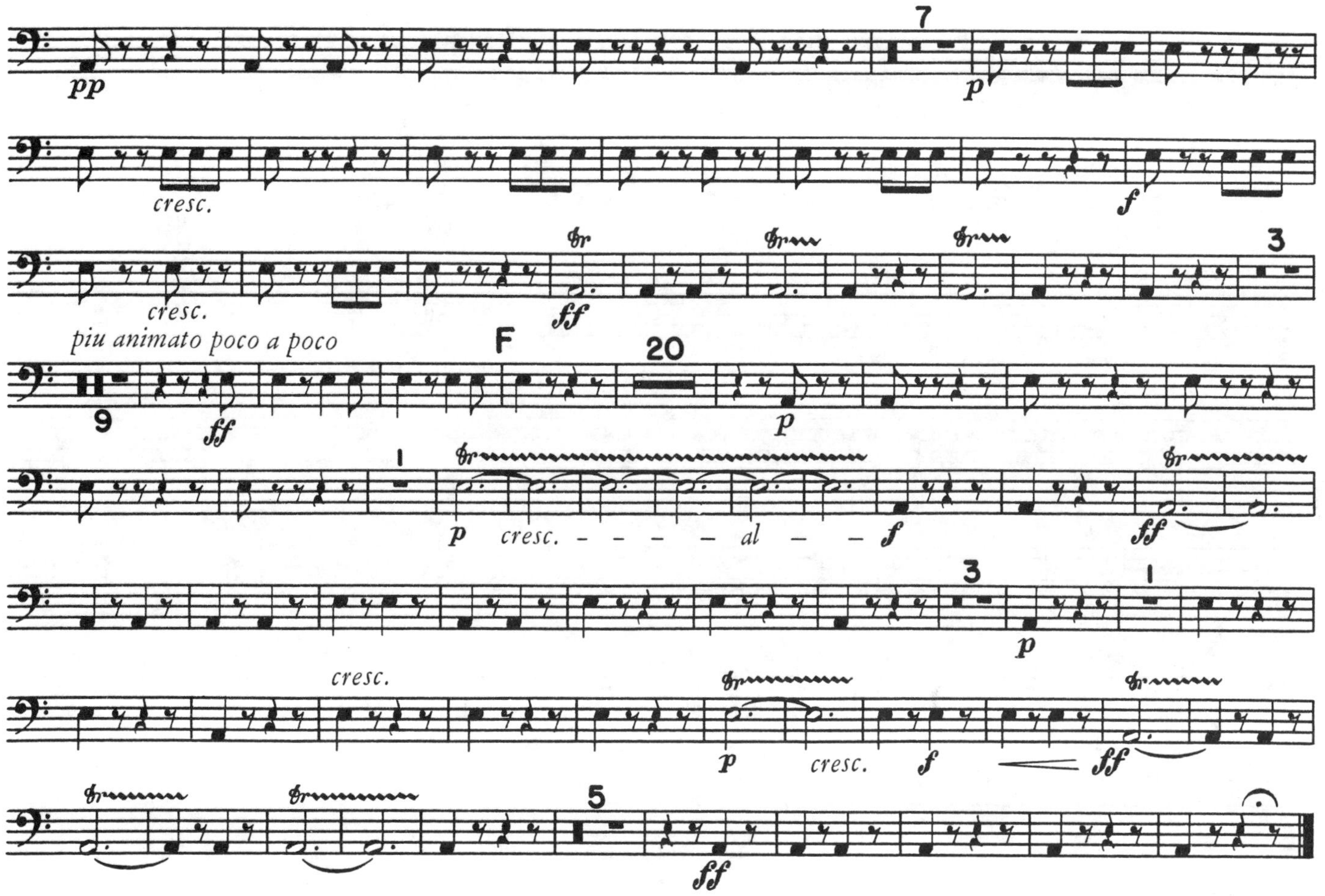
7
pp
p
cresc.
f
cresc.
ff
3
piu animato poco a poco
F
20
9
ff
p
1
p cresc. - - - - - al - - - f
ff
3
1
p
cresc.
p cresc. f ff
5
ff

Andante con moto *tacet*

Con moto moderato

in
E. H.
19
55
Corno
14
mf
2
2
cresc.
f
15
64
Viol.
65
66
67
68
69
8
Corni
1
p
2
9
pp
Presto
in E. A.
SALTARELLO
f
19
pp
1
2
3
4
3

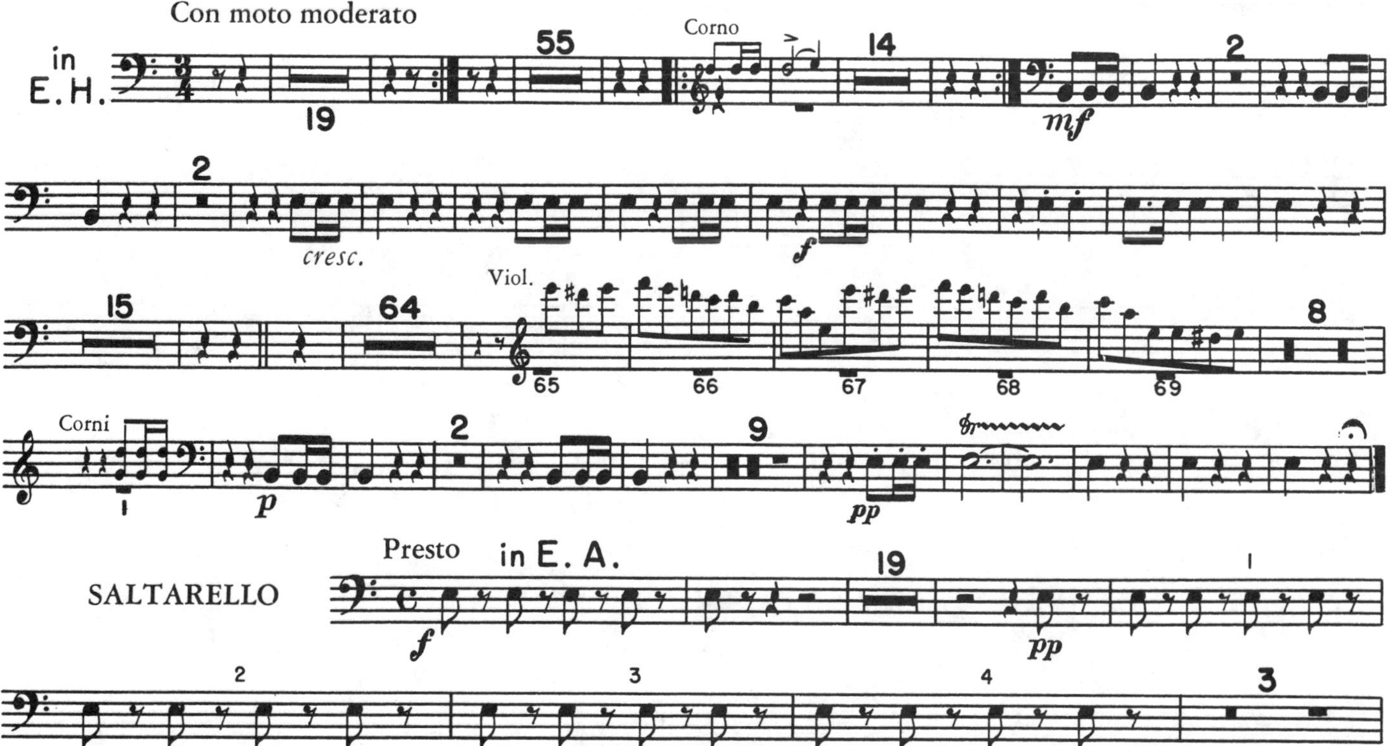

ff
9
f
2
ff
A
39
Viol.
40
41
42
43
44
ff
B
sf
47
Viol.
48
49
50
51
C
p
cresc.
cresc.
16
f
ff
ff
D
f
dimin.
p
cresc.
3
ff
f
5
f
E
3
p
dimin.
dimin.
11
pp
cresc.
f

Symphony No. 1

by JOHANNES BRAHMS, op. 68

259
268
decresc.
p
H
pp
276
284
I
K.-Fag. Vcl. K.-B.
296
pp
18
Trpt.
ff
K
321
329
sf
f
L
343
11
Ob. I
Viol. I
372
M
N
Ob. I
15
400
20
Klar. I
9
O
16
Hr. I
455
Trpt. I
464
471
P
Viol. I

Meno Allegro
p
p
p
p cresc. molto
f
p
in H, E
Andante sostenuto
Viol. I
Ob. I
Hr. I
pp
Viol. I
cresc.
p
Trpt. I
Viol. I
pp
Un poco Allegretto e grazioso tacet
in C, G
Adagio
K.-B.
f
p
pp
string. poco a poco
a tempo
Ob.
string. molto
a tempo
Klar. I
Hr. I
Trpt.
ff dim.
Più Andante
dim.

51
pp
cresc.
dim.
Allegro non troppo, ma con brio
62
Viol. I
Hr. I
sf
Fag.
p
79
90
cresc.
D
f
105
E
F
Klar. I
144
Viol. I
sf
151
p
G
168
f
179
H
192
I
Trpt.
Klar. I
215
K
244
L
Ob. I
Viol. I

M
268
f
276
282
N
ff
dim.
p
p marc. e cresc.
295
calando
dim.
animato
O
Viol.
320
Viol.
P
Viol. I
359
Trpt.
Viol. I
Q
375
string.
p
sf
cresc.
Più Allegro
391
mf
397
415
423
435
445
sf

Symphony No. 4

by JOHANNES BRAHMS, op. 98

O
pp
Viol.
P
f
ff
Q
Hr. III
mf
R
Trpt. I
Fl.
Ob.
Solo
in E, H
Andante moderato
Hr. III, IV
A
B
Trpt.
C
Fl.
Klar. I
D
Br.
p dolce
E
Holzbl. Hr.
Str.
Fag.
Klar.
F
Hr. I
ppp
rit.
a tempo
poco rit.
p
pp

in F, G, C
Allegro giocoso
ff
ffz
sf
A
Trpt. I
p cresc.
ff
B
Trgl.
C
Trgl.
Viol. I
p cresc.
D
ff
ff sempre
E
Str.
F
Hr. I
Fag. I
Poco meno presto
pp
dim.
pp
Klar. I
Tempo I
f
Trpt. I
p cresc.
ff
G
Viol. I
f

H
fpp
cresc.
I
ff sempre
K
Trgl.
in G, H, E
Allegro energico e passionato
Pos. III
dim.
A
B
Viol.
C
Viol.

Fl.
Ob.
fp
dim.
fp dim.
pp
Fl. Klar.
Klar. I
Ob.
Klar. I
Fl. I
Pos. III
ff
sf
Hr. III, IV
Bässe
p
f
Hr. I
pp
sf sempre
Viol. I
mf
poco ritard.
cresc.
Più Allegro
Pos.
cresc.
Pos. III

Symphony No. 4

by PETER ILYITCH TSCHAIKOWSKY, op. 36

*Change C to B and A to F♯ (see page 9).

(Timp. in H, Fis.)
Ben sostenuto il tempo precedente.
pp
G
stringendo poco a poco
crescendo
cres - - -
cen - - - do
po - - - co
a po
- co
H
crescendo
Moderato con anima.
f
fff
mf
mf
J
1
2
ff
ff
K
3
L (muta H in C e Fis in A)
4
5
fff
f
ff

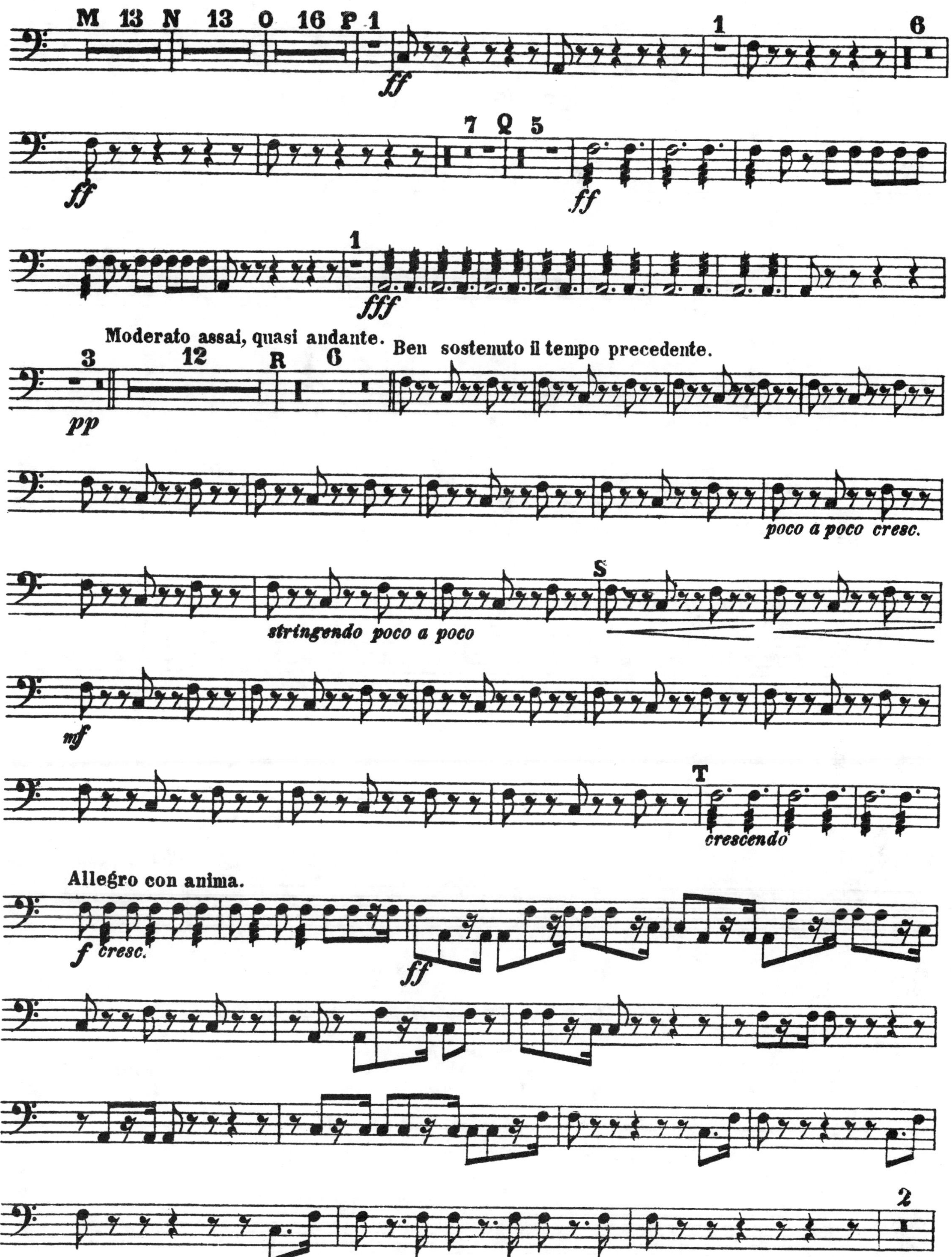

M 13 N 13 O 16 P 1
ff
1
6
ff
7 Q 5
ff
1
fff
Moderato assai, quasi andante.
3
12
R 6
pp
Ben sostenuto il tempo precedente.
poco a poco cresc.
S
stringendo poco a poco
mf
T
crescendo
Allegro con anima.
f cresc.
ff
2

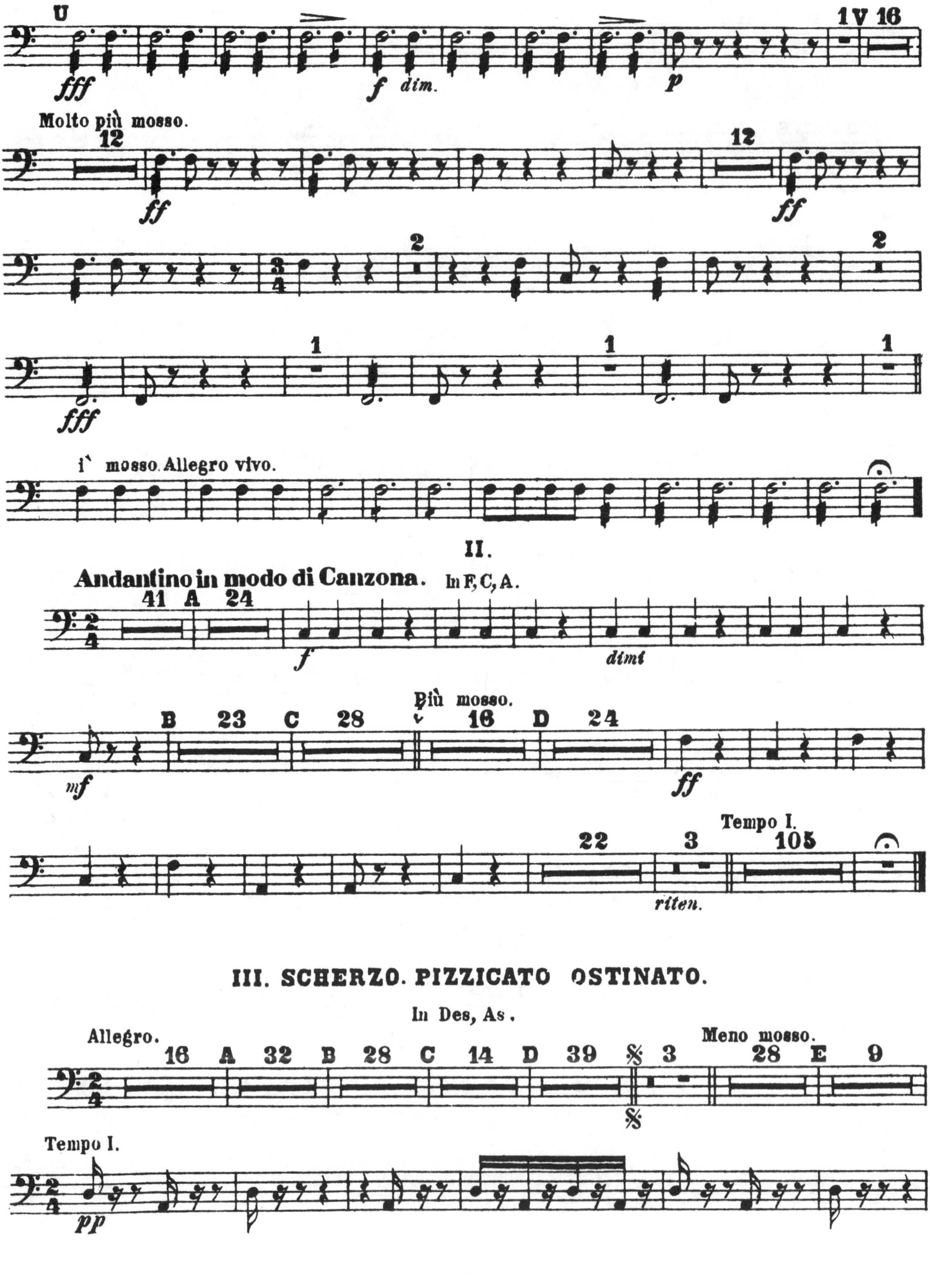

U fff f dim. p 1 V 16

Molto più mosso.

12 ff 12 ff

2 2 3/4

fff 1 1 1

i` mosso. Allegro vivo.

II.

Andantino in modo di Canzona. In F, C, A.

41 A 24 f dim.

Più mosso.

mf B 23 C 28 16 D 24 ff

Tempo I.

22 3 105 riten.

III. SCHERZO. PIZZICATO OSTINATO.

In Des, As.

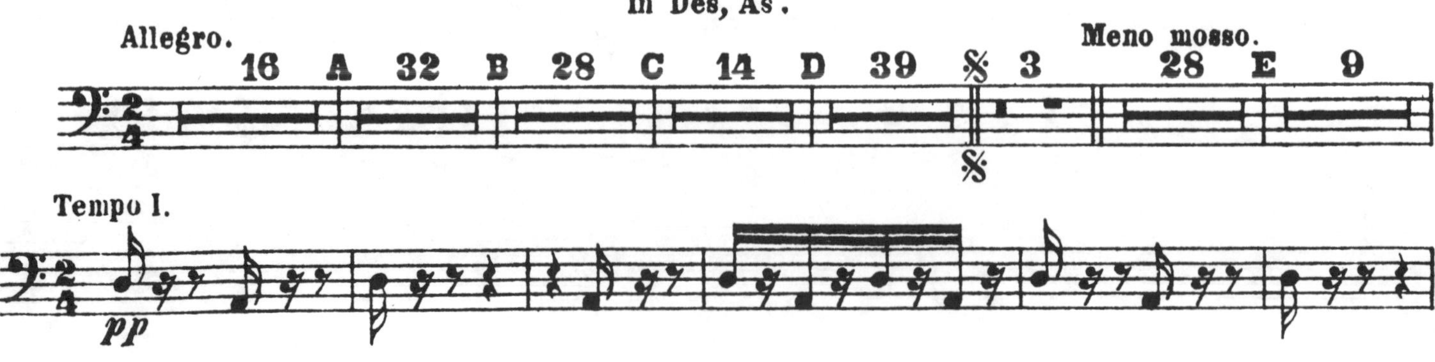

F
7
1
1G
3
7
Scherzo D. C. al segno e poi la Coda.
CODA.
H 18
J 34
mf
12
IV. FINALE.
Allegro con fuoco.
In F, C, G.
2
ff
2
21
A
ff
2
2
ff
3
5
B 32
C 27
D
fff
ff
2
2

ff
3
5
Andante. (𝅗𝅥=𝅗𝅥 предъидущаго)
E 24
F 26
6
1
14
fff
ff
Tempo I.
pp
cres - - cen - - do poco a po
co
G
f
4
2
fff
2
H
ffff
12
2
Fine.

Symphony No. 5

by PETER ILYITCH TSCHAIKOWSKY, op. 64

L 14
M
pp
ff
Muta A in G, D in B, E in D.
N 16
O
p poco a poco cresc.
P
Muta B in H, D in E.
Q 17 R 10
S
T 20
Poco meno animato. string. Tempo I.
U 12
Un pochettino più mosso. Molto più tranquillo come sopra.
18
V Viol. I.
string. Tempo I.
W
fff

X
14
f
Y
ff
p
pp
poco
a
poco
cresc.
Z
fff
ff
f
a
mp
p
b
pp
pp
ppp
1
1
ppp

II.

Tympani in Fis, Gis, D.

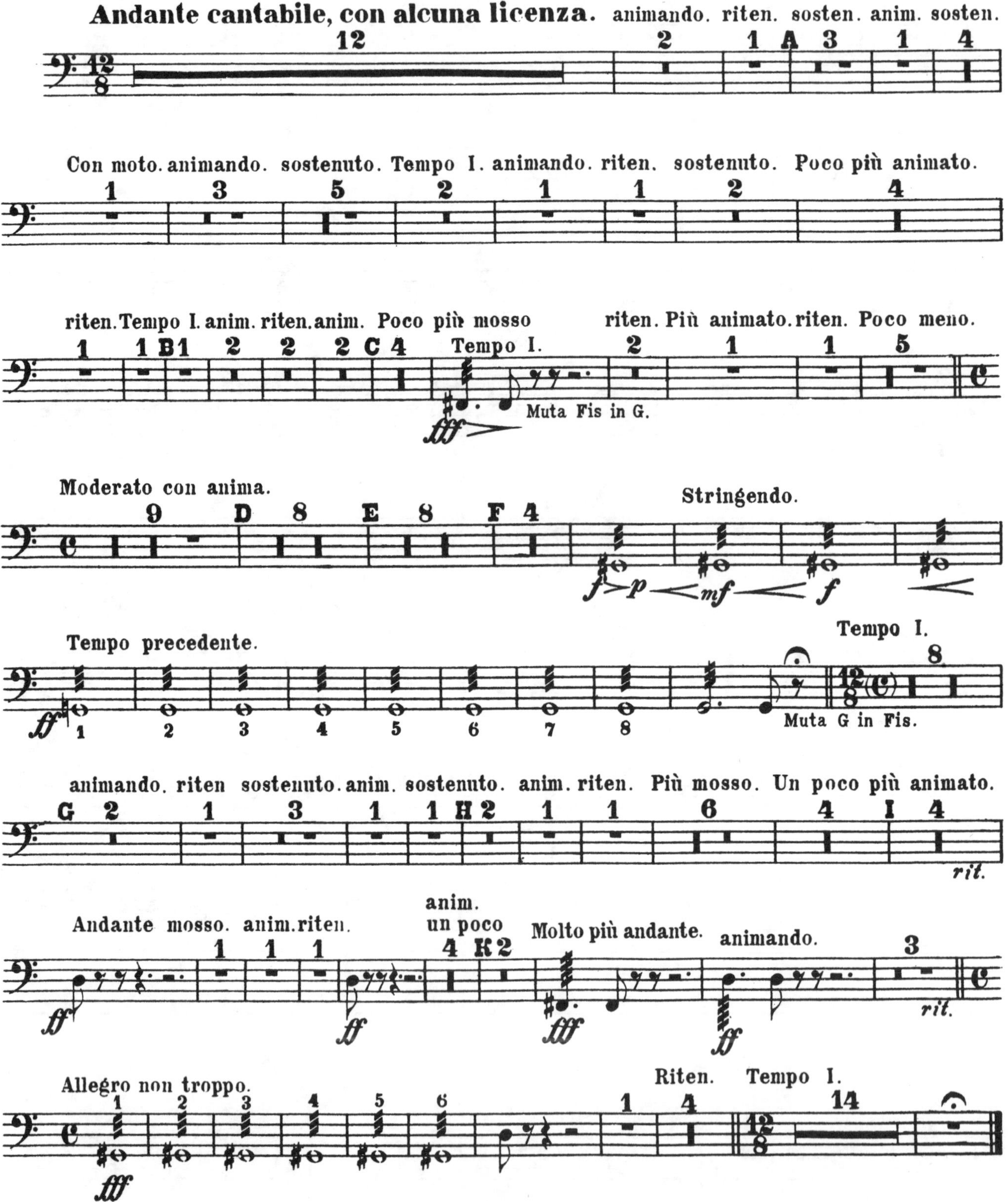

III.

VALSE.

Tympani in Fis, Cis.

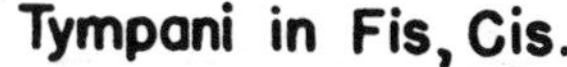

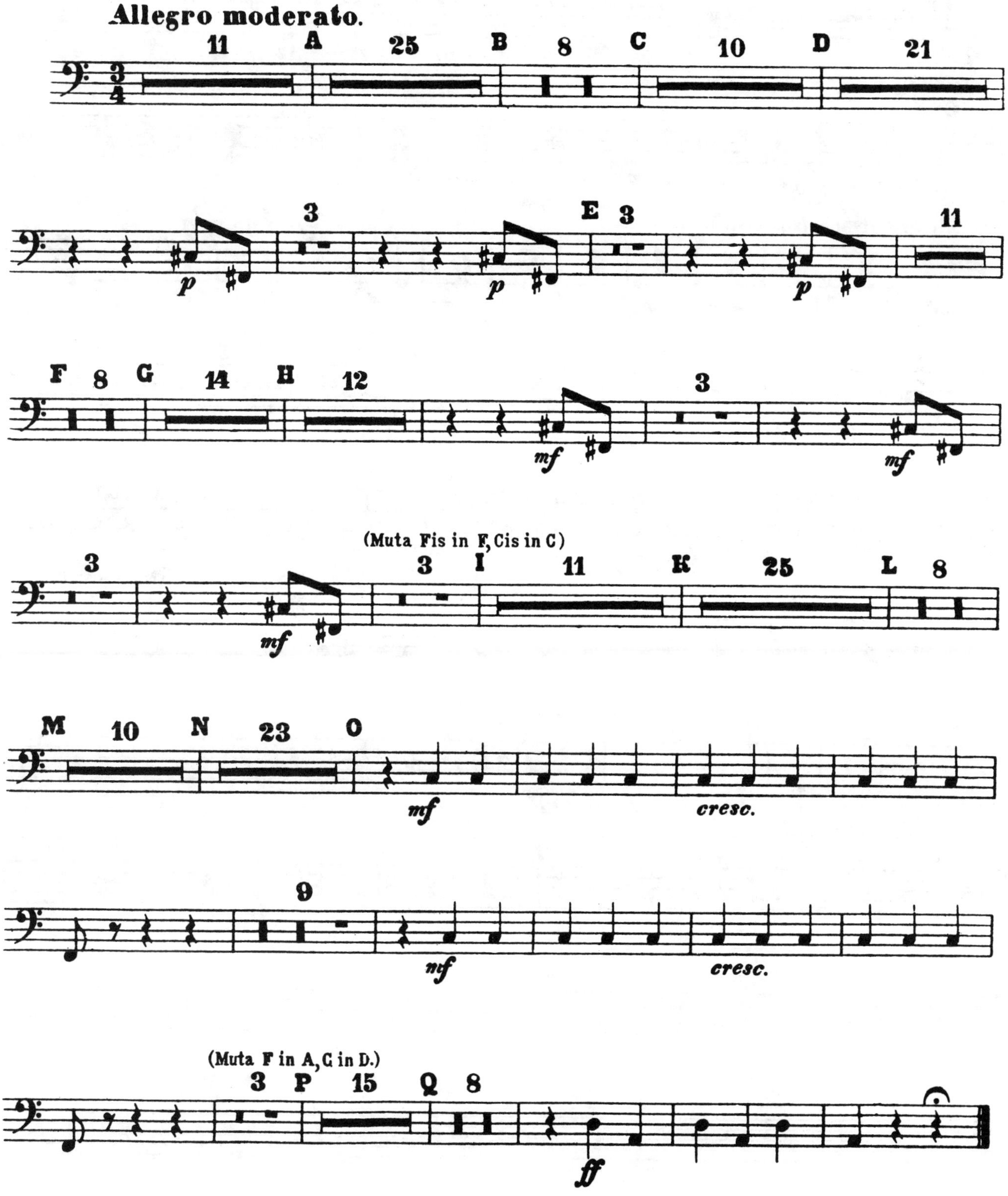
Allegro moderato.
(Muta Fis in F, Cis in C)
cresc.
cresc.
(Muta F in A, C in D.)

IV.

FINALE.

Tympani in G, C, E.

M
fff
f
N
ff
fff
11
O
27
P
24
Q
10
Fag I.
11
12
13
14
Poco piu animato.
ff
1
f
1
1
1
7
Tempo I.
3
ff
3
ff
1
(Muta G in A, C in H, E in Cis.)
R
ff
15
S
8
(in A, H, Cis.)
mf
T
p cresc.
ff
p cresc.
ff
mf
U
fff
dim.
pp
mf
(Muta A in Eis, Cis in E.)
11
V
8
W
16
X
8
Corno I.
9
10
11
in H. Fis. E.
Poco meno mosso.
mf
ff
mf
Molto vivace.
cresc.
ff
15
Y
fff
1
1
5

fff
Moderato assai e molto maestoso.
7
Z
8
f
a
fff
b
Presto.
5
c
10
sfff *sfff*
fff
d
3
fff
sempre fff
Molto meno mosso.
1
2
3
4
5
6
7
8
e

Finlandia

by JEAN SIBELIUS, op. 26 No. 7

Funeral Music

from DIE GÖTTERDÄMMERUNG by RICHARD WAGNER

1st & 2nd Tympani part Condensed by SAUL GOODMAN

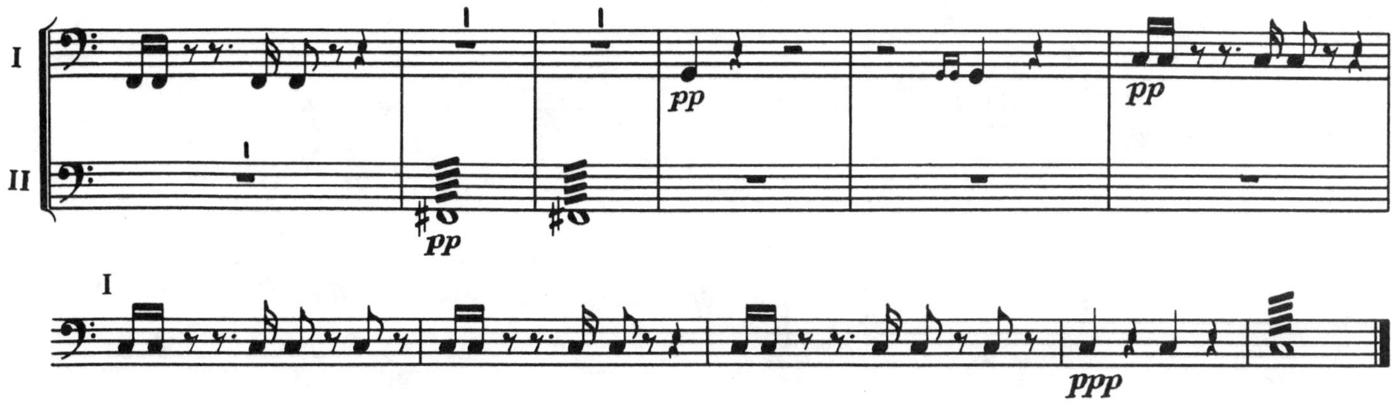

Symphonie Fantastique

by HECTOR BERLIOZ, op. 14

FOUR PLAYERS

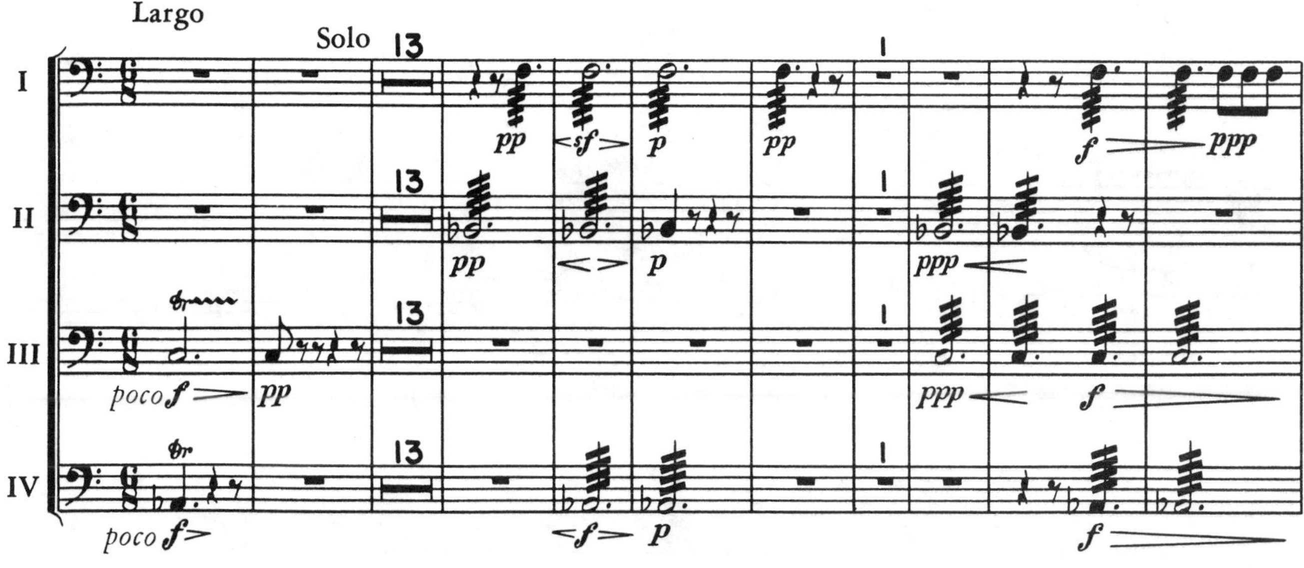

Till Eulenspiegels Lustige Streiche

by RICHARD STRAUSS, op. 28

drängend
steigern
mf molto cresc.
ff
17 ruhiger
pp
wütend
18 immer lebhafter
19
mit Holzschlägel.
fff
20
21
22 Vcell. u. Horn.
23
24
25
cresc.
accel.
26 leichtfertig.
longa
schnell und schattenhaft
27 Posaunen gedämpft.
28
poco rit. etwas gemächlicher
allmählich
Horn I.
lebhafter
Volles Zeitmass.
(sehr lebhaft.)
dim. pp
29
30

Tromb. I.
cresc.
immer ausgelassener und lebhafter
mit Holzschlägeln
mit Schwammschlägeln
etwas breiter
mf cresc.
kläglich
Epilog. Doppelt so langsam.
(im Zeitmass des Anfangs.)
Sehr lebhaft.
f cresc.

Schelomo

by ERNEST BLOCH

L'Oiseau de Feu

("Danse Infernale du Roi Katschei," "Berceuse" and "Finale")

by IGOR STRAWINSKY

Allegro agitato ♩ = 168

Avec des baguettes en bois

sfff pp subito Executez ces doubles croches avec deux mains—tres rythme!

sfff pp

sfff pp

sfff pp

sfff pp

sfff pp

Baguettes en bois

(Tuba)

f

en La♭, il Re♮

f

sfff pp sub.

Tamb. de Basque
p sentito
T.d.B.
Changez le La en mi
grave
in uno
Changez le mi aigu en Do, et le mi grave en Sol♯
Baguettes en bois
tres fort.
Baguettes ordin.
Berceuse and Finale
Lento maestoso
Tacet jasq'au
(Corno Solo)
(Arpe)
forte
meno f
piu f
sempre piu crescendo

Concerto For Violin And Orchestra

by PAUL HINDEMITH

A Stopwatch And An Ordnance Map

by SAMUEL BARBER, op. 15

William Billing's Overture

by WILLIAM H. SCHUMAN

Fugue in C Minor

by JOHANN SEBASTIAN BACH
Arr. by DIMITRI MITROPOULOS

Symphony No. 3

by WILLIAM H. SCHUMAN

American Salute

Based on "When Johnny Comes Marching Home"

by MORTON GOULD

Theme And Variations

by SAUL GOODMAN

Timpiana

by SAUL GOODMAN